HIS
NEEDS
HER
NEEDS

HIS NEEDS HER NEEDS

Building an Affair-Proof Marriage

Willard F. Harley, Jr.

 Fleming H. Revell

A Division of Baker Book House Co
Grand Rapids, Michigan 49516

© 1986, 1994, 2001 by Willard F. Harley, Jr.

Published by Fleming H. Revell
a division of Baker Book House Company
P.O. Box 6287, Grand Rapids, MI 49516-6287

Tenth printing, October 2004

Printed in the United States of America

Library of Congress Cataloging-in-Publication Data
Harley, Willard F.
  His needs, her needs : building an affair-proof marriage / Willard F. Harley, Jr.—15th anniversary ed.
     p.   cm.
   ISBN 0-8007-1788-0
   1. Marriage—United States. 2. Communication in marriage—United States. 3. Married people—United States—Psychology. I. Title.
HQ734.H285   2001
306.81'0973—dc21   00-067324

ISBN 0-8007-5779-3 (intl. pbk.)

To
Joyce—
my one and only

CONTENTS

PREFACE TO THE
15TH ANNIVERSARY EDITION

When I was nineteen, a married acquaintance in college told me his marriage was in trouble and asked for my advice. The advice I gave did not seem to help—his marriage ended in divorce. Why couldn't I help? What was it about my friend's marriage that made divorce seem so inevitable?

It was 1960, and I was about to witness something that few expected—the beginning of the end of the traditional nuclear family in America. Evidence of this disaster accumulated over the next twenty years. The divorce rate climbed from about 10 percent to over 50 percent, and the percentage of single adults would go from 6.5 percent to 20 percent. While the divorce rate finally stabilized at about 50 percent in 1980, the percentage of single adults has continued to climb right up to the present. It is currently at about 30 percent and climbing because fewer and fewer people are willing to commit themselves to one partner for life.

At the time, I didn't know that my friend's marital failure was part of a trend that was about to overwhelm nuclear families. I thought that his failure was, at least in part, due to my inexperience. I blamed myself. Thought I should not have tried to give advice. That I should have left it to an "expert."

But over the next few years, couples kept asking for my advice regarding marriage, especially after I earned a Ph.D. in psychology. After all, psychologists were supposed to know something about marriage. So I decided to learn enough to help these people. I didn't think it would be much of a challenge. After all, if our scientists knew enough to send people to the moon, surely they would know how to save marriages.

I read books on marital therapy, was supervised by "experts" in the field, and worked in a clinic that specialized in marital therapy and claimed to be the best in Minnesota. But I was still unable to save marriages. Almost everyone who came to me for help ended up like my college friend—divorced.

In my effort to overcome my own personal failure, I made a crucial discovery. I wasn't the only one failing to help couples. Almost everyone else working with me in the clinic was failing as well! My supervisor was failing, the director of the clinic was failing, and so were the other marriage counselors who worked with me.

And then I made the most astonishing discovery of all. *Most of the marital experts in America were also failing.* It was very difficult to find anyone willing to admit their failure, but when I had access to actual cases, I couldn't find any therapist who could prove their success or train others to be successful in saving marriages.

In fact, I learned that marital therapy had the lowest success rate of any form of therapy. In one study, I read that less than 25 percent of those surveyed felt that marriage counseling did them any good whatsoever, and a higher percentage felt that it did them more harm than good. (Incidentally, as recently as 1995, a Consumer's Report study of psychotherapy reported that marital therapy is still rated lowest in effectiveness).

What a challenge! Marriages were breaking up at an unprecedented rate, and no one knew how to stop it. So I made it my own personal ambition to find the answer, and I looked for that answer not in books and scholarly articles but among those who came to me for answers—couples about to divorce.

I stopped counseling and started listening to spouses explain why they were ready to throw in the towel. What did they have when they decided to marry that they lost somewhere along the way. I asked them, "What do you think it would take for you to be happily married again?"

I knew that I had not yet learned how to save marriages, so I explained that inability to the couples I counseled. And, appropriately, I did not charge any of them for my time. I taught psychology to earn a living and talked with couples in my office on a part-time basis. And my policy of free, albeit ineffective, counseling provided me with more troubled couples than I had time to see.

By 1975 I had discovered why I and so many other therapists were having trouble saving marriages. We did not understand what made marriages work. We were all so preoccupied with what seemed to make them fail that we overlooked what made them succeed. Whenever a couple would come to my office, they would be making each other miserable. So I thought, as most others thought, that if I could simply get them to communicate more clearly, resolve their conflicts more effectively, and stop fighting with each other so much, that their marriage would be saved. But that wasn't the answer.

Couple after couple explained to me that they didn't marry each other because they communicated so clearly or resolved their conflicts effectively or didn't fight. They married each other because they found each other irresistible—they were in love. But by the time they came to my office they had lost that feeling of love. In fact, many were finding each other downright repulsive. And one of the primary reasons that they were communicating so poorly, resolving their conflicts so ineffectively, and fighting so much, was that they had lost that feeling of love.

When I asked the question, "What would it take for you to be happily married again?" most couldn't imagine that ever happening. But when I persisted and couples were able to reflect on my question, the answer I heard repeated over and over was, "for us to be in love again."

Granted, poor communication, failure to resolve conflicts, and fighting all contribute to the loss of love. But they are also symptoms of lost love. In other words, if I wanted to save marriage, I would have to go beyond improving communication. I would have to learn how to restore love.

With this insight I began to attack emotional issues rather than rational issues. My primary goal in marital therapy changed from resolving conflicts to restoring love. If I knew how to restore love, I reasoned, then communication, conflict resolution, and fighting might not be as much of a problem.

My background as a psychologist taught me that learned associations trigger most of our emotional reactions. Whenever something is presented repeatedly with a physically induced emotion, it tends to trigger that emotion all by itself. For example, if you flash the color blue along with an electric shock, and the color red with a soothing back rub, eventually the color blue will tend to upset you and the color red will tend to relax you.

Applying the same principle to the feeling of love, I theorized that love might be nothing more than a learned association. If someone were to be present often enough when I was feeling particularly good, the person's presence in general might be enough to trigger that good feeling—something we have come to know as the feeling of love.

I could not have been more correct in my analysis. By encouraging each spouse to try to do whatever it took to make each other happy and avoid doing what made each other unhappy, that feeling of love was restored with the very next couple I counseled. Their marriage was saved.

From that point on, each time I saw a couple, I simply asked them what the other could do that would make them the happiest, and whatever it was, that was their first assignment. Of course, not every couple really knew what would make them happy, and not every spouse was willing to do it. So I certainly wasn't successful with every couple.

But as I perfected my approach to this problem, I began to understand what it was that husbands and wives needed from each other to trigger the feeling of love, and I helped them identify what each of them needed. I also became more effective in motivating them to meet whatever need was identified, even when they didn't feel like it at first.

Before long, I was helping almost every couple fall in love and thereby avoid divorce. My method proved to be so successful, that I quit teaching psychology, and started counseling full-time. As you can imagine, there were more couples wanting help from me than I could possibly counsel.

Ten years after I began using this method, I finally wrote my first book describing it, *His Needs, Her Needs: Building an Affair-Proof Marriage*. And now, fifteen years after the first copy came off the press, over one million copies have been printed and it has been translated into eleven languages. Many have called it the best book on marriage ever written. That may be true, because as far as I know it is still the only book written that provides a tried and proven plan for married couples to restore and sustain their love for each other.

What makes this book so effective is that it gets right to the heart of what makes marriages work—the feeling of love. Communication and problem-solving skills are important in a happy marriage, but not absolutely essential. It's the feeling of love that's absolutely essential. In all my years as a marriage counselor, I've never counseled a couple in love who wanted a divorce. But I've counseled many divorcing couples with excellent communication and problem-solving skills.

Don't get me wrong—I'm very much in favor of improving communication and problem solving in marriage. But unless those skills help trigger the feeling of love, spouses feel cheated in their marriages and often want out.

This book will teach you what's most important in marriage—how to fall in love and stay in love with each other. I encourage you and your spouse to read this book together, complete the questionnaires, and answer the questions at the end of each chapter. You might even use two different colored highlighters as you read so each of you can let the other know what is most important to you.

I have received letters from scores of couples who have dedicated each New Year's Day to re-reading *His Needs, Her Needs* as a reminder of what they must do in the coming year to keep their marriage passionate. And it works. This is a book to be read often, because it's about being skilled in meeting each other's most important emotional needs.

Introduction

Marital conflict is created one of two ways: (1) Couples *fail to make* each other *happy*, or (2) couples make each other *unhappy*. In the first case, couples are frustrated because their needs are not being met. In the second case, they're deliberately hurting each other. I call the first cause of conflict *failure to care* and the second, *failure to protect*.

This book addresses the failure to care—failure to meet each other's most important emotional needs. Ignorance contributes to this failure because men and women have great difficulty understanding and appreciating the value of each other's needs. Men tend to try to meet needs that they would value and women do the same. The problem is that the needs of men and women are often very different and we waste effort trying to meet the wrong needs.

The right needs are so strong that when they're not met in marriage, people are tempted to go outside marriage to satisfy them. And most of the people I've counseled have yielded to the temptation to violate their sacred vow to "forsake all others."

But aside from the risk of an affair, important emotional needs *should be met* for the sake of care itself. Marriage is a very special relationship. Promises are made to allow a spouse the *exclusive* right to meet some of these important needs. When they are unmet, that is unfair to the spouse who must go through life without ethical alternatives.

This book will help couples to identify these important needs, to communicate them to each other, and to learn to meet them.

The second cause of marital conflict, failure to protect, is the subject of a companion book I've written, *Love Busters: Overcoming the Habits That Destroy Romantic Love*. Couples that find their needs unmet often become thoughtless and inconsiderate. When that happens, marriages slide into ugly and destructive scenes. The failure to meet these needs is often unintentional, but reaction to unmet needs develops into *intentional* harm. That often leads to unbearable pain and, ultimately, divorce.

To help couples overcome marital conflict, my strategy focuses on both causes of conflict: the failure to care and the failure to protect. This book and its companion volume will help you create a marriage that is fulfilling and safe.

The exercises mentioned in both books refer to forms I use in my counseling practice. While many of these forms are printed in this book, all of them are available in *Five Steps to Romantic Love: A Workbook for a Healthy Marriage for Readers of Love Busters* and *His Needs, Her Needs*. Any husband and wife who are serious about improving their marriage will benefit from working through all of the worksheets in this workbook.

Successful marriages require skill—skill in caring for the one you promised to cherish throughout life. Good intentions are not enough. *This book was written to educate you in the care of your spouse.* Once you have learned its lessons, your spouse will find you irresistible, a condition that is essential to a happy and successful marriage.

1

How Affair-Proof Is Your Marriage?

I've written this book for those who want to be happily married. Whether you have just started your life together, have had a mediocre marriage for a number of years, or have had a horrible marriage, you can have a happy marriage if you learn to:

> Become aware
> of each other's emotional needs
> and learn to meet them.

This is a simple statement, but applying this principle to the complexities of marriage requires some careful thought. Let's take a look at what it really involves.

When a man and woman marry, they share high expectations. They commit themselves to meeting certain intense and intimate needs in each other on an *exclusive* basis. Each agrees to "forsake all others," giving each other the exclusive right to meet these intimate needs. That does not imply that all needs are to be met by a spouse, but that there are a few basic needs that most of us strictly reserve for the marriage bond. Most people expect their spouses to meet these special needs, since they have agreed not to allow anyone else to meet them.

For example, when a man agrees to an exclusive relationship with his wife, he depends on her to meet his sexual need. If she fulfills this need, he finds in her a continuing source of intense pleasure, and his love grows stronger. However, if his need goes unmet, quite the opposite happens. He begins to associate her with frustration. If the frustration continues, he may decide she "just doesn't like sex" and may try to make the best of it. But his strong need for sex remains unfulfilled. His commitment to an exclusive sexual relationship with his wife has left him with the choice of sexual frustration or infidelity. Some men never give in; they manage to make the best of it over the years. But many *do* succumb to the temptation of an affair. I have talked to hundreds of them in my counseling offices.

Another example is a wife who gives her husband the exclusive right to meet her need for intimate conversation. Whenever they talk together with a depth of honesty and openness not found in conversation with others, she finds him to be the source of her greatest pleasure. But when he refuses to give her the undivided attention she craves, he becomes associated with her greatest frustration. Some women simply go through their married lives frustrated, but others cannot resist the temptation to let someone else meet this important emotional need. And when they do, an affair is the likely outcome.

His Needs Are Not Hers

When a husband and wife come to me for help, my first goal is to help them identify their most important emotional needs—what each of them can do for each other to make them happiest and most content. Over the years, I have repeatedly asked the question, "What could your spouse do for you that would make you the happiest?" I've been able to classify most of their responses into ten emotional needs— admiration, affection, conversation, domestic support, family commitment, financial support, honesty and openness, physical attractiveness, recreational companionship, and sexual fulfillment.

Obviously the way to keep a husband and wife happily married is for each of them to meet the needs that are most important to the other. But when I conducted all these interviews I discovered why that is such a difficult assignment. Nearly every time I asked couples to list their needs according to their priority, men listed them one way and women the opposite way. Of the ten basic emotional needs, the five listed as most important by men were usually the five least important for women, and vice versa.

What an insight! No wonder husbands and wives have so much difficulty meeting each other's needs. They are willing to do for each other what they appreciate the most, but it turns out that their efforts are misdirected because what they appreciate most, their spouses appreciate least!

Pay careful attention to this next point I'm about to make, because it's one of the most misunderstood aspects of my program. Every person is unique. While men *on the average* pick a particular five emotional needs as their most important and women *on the average* pick another five, *any individual* can and does pick any combination of the basic ten. So although I have identified the most important emotional needs of the average man and woman, I don't know the emotional needs of any particular husband and wife. And since I'm in the business of saving individual marriage, not average marriages, you need to identify the combinations of needs that are unique to your marriage. I have provided a brief summary of the ten basic needs in appendix A and the Emotional Needs Questionnaire in appendix B. This will help you identify the most important emotional needs unique to you and your spouse.

Often the failure of men and women to meet each other's emotional needs is simply due to ignorance of each other's needs and not selfish unwillingness to be considerate. Fulfilling those needs does not mean you have to painfully grit your teeth, making the best of something you hate. It means preparing yourself to meet needs you may not appreciate yourself. By learning to understand your spouse as a totally different person than you, you can begin to become an expert in meeting all that person's emotional needs.

In marriages that fail to meet those needs, I have seen, strikingly and alarmingly, how married people consistently choose the same pattern to satisfy their unmet needs: the extramarital affair. People wander into affairs with astonishing regularity, in spite of whatever strong moral or religious convictions they may hold. Why? Once a spouse lacks fulfillment of any of the five needs, it creates a thirst that must be quenched. If changes do not take place within the marriage to care for that need, the individual will face the powerful temptation to fill it outside of marriage.

In order to make our marriages affair-proof, we cannot hide our heads in the sand. The spouse who believes his or her partner is "different" and, despite unmet needs, would never take part in an affair may receive a devastating shock someday. Instead, we need to understand the warning signs that an affair could happen, how such liaisons may begin, and how to strengthen the weak areas of a marriage in the face of such a relationship.

What Is an Affair?

An affair usually consists of two people who become involved in an extramarital relationship that combines sexual lovemaking with feelings of deep love. However, it is possible to have an affair with only lovemaking or with only the feeling of love towards someone outside of marriage. Although these types of affairs may also cause deep problems in marriage, my experience shows that they are more easily dealt with than the relationship that combines sex (usually very passionate sex) with very real love. That relationship threatens the marriage to its core, because the lovers experience real intimacy, and it meets at least one emotional need of the spouse outside the exclusive marital relationship. In most cases, when one spouse discovers the other has broken the commitment of faithfulness, the marriage is shattered.

Affairs Usually Start by "Just Being Friends"

An affair usually begins as a friendship. Frequently your spouse knows your lover; not uncommonly the third party is the husband or wife in a couple you both know and consider "best friends." In another common pattern the outside lover comes from your spouse's family—a sister or brother. Or you may have met your lover at work.

When an affair starts, it usually begins as a friendship. You share problems with the other person, and that person shares problems with you. Usually, for the affair to blossom, you have to see this other person quite often: every day at work or frequently through a friendship, being on a committee or board, or some other responsibility that brings you together.

As your friendship deepens, you start giving each other mutual support and encouragement, especially in regard to your unmet needs. Life is difficult. Many people become extremely disillusioned about their lives. When they find someone encouraging and supportive, the attraction toward that person acts as a powerful magnet. Sooner or later, you find yourself in bed with your encouraging and supportive friend. It just seems to "happen." You don't intend it, and neither does your friend.

Very often the friendship that grows into an affair is not based on physical attraction. A wife will get a look at her husband's lover and exclaim, "How in the world could he be interested in *her?*"

The answer is, "Very easily," because the attraction is emotional. It doesn't necessarily matter if the other woman is overweight, plain, or really rather ugly. What matters is that she has been able to meet an unfulfilled need. The lover in an affair often turns out to be regarded as the most caring person the wayward spouse has ever met. The straying spouse develops a reciprocal desire to care for the lover at a depth never before experienced.

When you become caught in an affair, you and your lover share a strong willingness to meet each other's needs. This willingness binds you in a mutual love that develops into a passionate sexual relationship. This mutual desire to bring each other happiness builds an affair into one of the most satisfying and intimate relationships either of you have ever known.

As the intensity of your mutual care and passion increases, you discover yourself caught in a trap of your own making. You lose all sense of judgment as you literally become addicted to each other in a relationship built upon fantasy, not reality.

Several factors contribute to making an affair so enjoyable and exciting:

- You and your lover seem to bring out the best in each other.
- You ignore each other's faults.
- You get turned on sexually as never before. You feel sure no one else could ever be as exciting a sex partner as your secret new lover.

What really turns you on, however, is not your new partner, but the fantasy. As you and your lover plan where and when to meet for passionate sessions of lovemaking you leave the realities of living behind. Your affair may go on for quite a while before anyone detects it. The longer it goes on, the more difficult you will find breaking it off.

As I've discussed affairs and how they start, I may have offended you, at least a little bit, by using the second-person pronoun. But I used *you* for a specific reason. While most people would deny they could ever get involved in an affair, the hard truth is that, under the right (or wrong) conditions, any of us can fall victim, if our basic needs are not being met.

It doesn't take something different or special to fall into an affair. On the contrary, sometimes very normal men and women get involved in one through a deceptively simple process. When your basic needs go unmet, you start thinking, *This isn't right. It isn't fair.*

Next you start looking for support and find yourself saying, *If only I had someone to talk to.*

From there it can only be a short step to looking for support outside your exclusive marriage bond. You don't necessarily go hunting for this person; he or she just turns up, and you find yourself saying, "Isn't it great how we can just talk and share together?"

In some cases the above process may take only a few months; in other cases it will take many years. But it can happen. I have seen it happening in the lives of my clients for the last twenty-five years. Sadly enough, it seems to make little difference what a person professes by way of religious commitment or moral values.

Early in my career as a counselor I often felt dismayed to see people with strong religious and moral commitments becoming involved in extramarital affairs. I am a church member myself, with strong convictions about the Christian faith. How could people who claim to have the same commitments go astray? Did their faith lack power?

The more I dealt with Christian clients and other people with deep moral convictions, the more I understood the power of our basic emotional needs. I came to see my own weaknesses and the strength of my own needs. When I married my wife, Joyce, I determined to be totally committed to her and to my marriage. I have remained true to my vows for the thirty-eight years of our marriage, but not because I am some kind of iron-willed paragon of virtue. It's because Joyce and I have been realistic about meeting each other's important emotional needs.

In short, your needs keep score. To help you understand how this works, I'd like to introduce you to the Love Bank—an inner scoring device you probably never realized you had.

2

WHY YOUR LOVE BANK
NEVER CLOSES

Marriage is a complex relationship, perhaps the most intricate of them all. Unfortunately, most of us don't realize what we're getting into when we say, "I do." We think the dynamics of a good marriage depend on some mysterious blend of the "right" people. Or if a marriage turns out badly, we call the two people "wrong" for each other. While it's true that two inherently incompatible people *might* marry, it's unusual. More frequently, marital breakups occur when one or both partners lack the skills or awareness to meet each other's needs. More often than not, being right or wrong for someone depends not on some mysterious compatibility quotient, but on how willing and able you are to meet that someone's needs.

What, then, if you are willing but unable or unskilled? Good news! You can do something about it. Retraining is possible at any time. For that reason I believe marriages that have been torpedoed by affairs need not sink. They can be towed into drydock, repaired, and refitted. Once refitted, they will sail farther and faster than at any previous time.

But my goal is not limited to salvaging marriages that have gone on the rocks of an affair. I reach well beyond that. I want to show you how to affair-proof your marriage by building a relationship that sustains romance and increases intimacy and closeness year after year. In order to make your marriage affair-proof, you need to know each other's basic needs and how to meet them. But first I want to help you understand how needs become so powerful and all-consuming. As I said in the first chapter, needs keep score with relentless precision. To help my clients understand how this scorekeeping works, I have invented a concept that I call the Love Bank.

Everyone Has a Love Bank

Figuratively speaking, I believe each of us has a Love Bank. It contains many different accounts, one for each person we know. Each person either makes deposits or withdrawals whenever we interact with him or her. Pleasurable interactions cause deposits, and painful interactions cause withdrawals.

In my Love Bank system every deposit or withdrawal is worth a certain number of love units. If I meet a friend (we'll call him Jim), and the encounter leaves me feeling comfortable, one love unit will be deposited in his account in my Love Bank. If the interchange makes me feel good, Jim's deposit in my bank is two love units. Very good gets three. Four units go to him when he makes me feel exceptionally good.

Suppose, however, that I find myself feeling uncomfortable when I am with someone; we'll call her Jane. One love unit is withdrawn from Jane's account. If she makes me feel bad, two units are withdrawn. Very bad warrants a three-unit withdrawal. If I consider my encounter with Jane among the worst experiences of my life, it costs her a four-unit withdrawal.

As life goes on the accounts in my Love Bank fluctuate. Some of my acquaintances build sizable deposits. Others remain in the black, but have small balances, perhaps because of fewer interactions with me. A third group builds up still smaller balances because my experiences with them are mixed, sometimes pleasant, sometimes painful. For these people, deposits almost equal withdrawals.

Other people go into the red with me. That means they cause me more pain than pleasure. I never feel good when I think of them, and I do not want to see them or be with them. In short, their accounts at my Love Bank are overdrawn.

A Love-Bank Love Story

Obviously, the Love Bank is not intended to be a mathematically accurate concept. It is simply designed to underscore the fact that we affect each other emotionally with almost every encounter. The accumulation of positive and negative experiences determines our emotional reaction to those we know. You are not actively aware of any of this, of course. You don't say to yourself, *Wow, that was a three-unit deposit!* or, *Ugh! Minus four units for him.* Nonetheless, the love units keep coming in or going out.

Two Love Banks constantly operate in marriage: his and hers. Let's take a look at the story of John and Mary to see what can happen when a wife's account in her husband's Love Bank takes a huge dip and there is an understanding woman waiting in the wings down at hubby's office. In this example, we will concentrate on John's Love Bank, because he winds up having the affair.

When John meets Mary, he immediately feels something special. Not only is she beautiful, but she is charming, intelligent, and full of life. John's Love Bank instantly credits her account with three units.

A day or two later John calls Mary and asks her for a date. She accepts, and as John hangs up, two more units go into Mary's account.

On the date they have a fabulous time. John rates it as one of the best experiences of his life. Four more units added to Mary's account brings her balance to nine love units. A second date is almost as good, and she gets three more love units, bringing the balance to twelve.

But the next time John calls Mary for a date, she has to turn him down. She says she feels truly sorry, but she has a commitment she set up many weeks ago. She quickly adds that she is free the next night, if John would be interested. John is indeed interested and arranges to pick her up for dinner about eight o'clock.

What happens to Mary's account in John's Love Bank as a result of this slightly negative encounter?

She definitely sounded sorry she couldn't go out with me tonight, John muses. *I can't expect her to be available just any time. Besides, she did suggest that we go out tomorrow night. I'm sure she really likes me. . . .*

No matter how much John tries to assure himself, the experience still leaves him feeling slightly uncomfortable. Mary's account in John's Love Bank is debited for one unit.

Over the next few months John and Mary date regularly and often. The good and fabulous experiences far outnumber the occasional negative ones, and Mary's balance soon stands at 250 love units. Only Sarah, an old flame whom John broke off with over a year ago, had ever accumulated more units in John's Love Bank. John begins to believe he is falling in love with Mary.

After six more months, Mary's balance stands at 500 love units, an all-time high total for any woman in John's life, well in excess of Sarah's score. At this point John feels he has never loved anyone as much as he loves Mary. He tells her she is the most attractive, intelligent, sensitive, charming, and delightful woman he has ever met.

Mary appeals to John so because of her balance in his Love Bank. He associates her with many positive—even fabulous—emotional experiences and only a few negative ones. John looks forward to each date with Mary, and his mind dwells on her when they are apart.

John begins to wonder what he would do if he ever lost Mary. He can't imagine going through the rest of his life without her.

With Mary at my side, I wouldn't need anything or anyone else in order to be happy, John tells himself. Vivid thoughts of marriage form in his mind.

Meanwhile, John's account in Mary's Love Bank has grown steadily, but not at quite the same pace. When they met, Mary found John quite attractive. The first dates were very good experiences, and at this point she feels quite fond of him, but she still isn't sure. Mary remembers Bob, and how fond she had been of him before he had broken off with her to marry an old friend from high school.

On their next date Mary abruptly tells John she needs a little breathing room. She suggests that they suspend their dating for a month or so and wonders if they shouldn't date other people during that time.

John feels devastated. This encounter registers as one of the all-time painful experiences of his life. Four units quickly come out of Mary's hefty account. A few days later John calls Mary and tries to convince her to change her mind, but she remains resolute. John tries calling back several times over the next week. Mary stands fast, and before John decides to leave her alone for a month, debits in Mary's account total twenty-five.

John spends the month feeling miserable. He remains deeply in love with Mary whose balance in his Love Bank still stands high, at 471 units. John tries to date several other women, but they do not stand a chance. Because he is so crazy about Mary, he finds dating any other girl a negative experience. Through no fault of their own, all of John's dates accumulate nothing but debits in their accounts.

At the end of a month, John calls Mary. Her balance has remained at 471, because, while he has pined for her, there have been no further negative experiences to cause any more withdrawals. John feels ecstatic when Mary tells him that she has missed him terribly and accepts his invitation to a date the very next evening. All she needed, she says, was time to think things through and see clearly how she felt.

The first date after the month-long separation is a memorable experience. Subsequent dates seem better than ever. At the end of the year, Mary's balance in John's Love Bank has risen to 1,000 units. At the same time, John's account in Mary's Love Bank has risen steadily and is at an all-time high of 925 units. John has eclipsed Bob in every way and Mary also thinks of wedding bells.

One night, after dinner at their favorite restaurant, John proposes marriage. He tells Mary he wants to live his life for her happiness and assures her that if she will marry him, he will never do anything to hurt her. She accepts his proposal, and after a brief engagement, they become man and wife.

Beyond the Honeymoon

The first year of their marriage is an extremely happy one. Without really thinking about it, John and Mary meet each other's basic needs quite well. John remains affectionate, patient, and as caring as he was when they dated. Mary responds passionately during lovemaking. They spend considerable time together and share their hopes and dreams in long conversations. Mary takes tennis lessons so that she can keep up with John in his favorite recreational pastime.

Mary knows she can trust John, because he is so honest in everything. John is proud of his attractive wife and feels particularly pleased with how she handles details around the house while still keeping her secretarial job on a part-time basis. John earns an excellent income as a computer analyst, but he and Mary have agreed she should work as much as she likes, at least for the present.

Mary feels secure with John, who gives every indication he loves being settled down with a home and family. She feels proud of John and often tells him so.

During their first year of married bliss, what happens to the balances in each partner's Love Bank? Interestingly enough John and Mary do not accumulate points at the rate they did before the marriage, mainly because they share a much wider variety of experiences than they had while dating. Now they are together when they feel good and when they feel bad. Credits and debits in their Love Bank accounts are being posted in accordance with the ups and downs of life.

In spite of her reduced rate of earnings in the Love Bank, Mary's balance in John's Love Bank still increases. At the end of their first year of marriage, her net gain from the previous year adds up to a hundred units. That brings her overall total to 1,100. Approximately the same pattern holds true for John. During the next four years accounts in both Love Banks continue to rise.

On their fifth anniversary, John still feels madly in love with Mary, and she feels the same about him. They decide to start a family, and little Tiffany arrives as they start their sixth year of marriage.

Critical changes start taking place in that sixth year. Mary is still the joy of John's life, but he notices an increase in his "down times." While Tiffany is a little doll and John loves her dearly, she still creates new demands and negative experiences. Taking his turn to change baby's diaper in the middle of the night is not John's idea of a pleasant time. Also Mary's decision not to nurse Tiffany leaves John with his share of responsibilities to walk with her and hold the bottle. In addition Mary has a tough time losing the weight she gained while she was pregnant.

As a net result of all these common little vicissitudes, Mary's balance in John's Love Bank drops by a hundred points over the year. The loss is not that significant—yet. Mary's balance still remains very high, and John feels deeply in love with her.

But around the time of Tiffany's second birthday, Mary gets restless. She wants to be more than just a part-time secretary. She wants to have a more important career and doesn't want to wait until all of her children are grown and gone. She asks John if he would object if she returned to college, finished her bachelor's degree, and possibly went on for a master's in business administration.

"It will take six years of classes," Mary explains. "But I'll quit my part-time job so I can concentrate on the baby during the day and take most of the classwork at night."

John agrees to her idea enthusiastically. He enjoys a solid and stable income by now, and they don't really need Mary's paycheck. He offers to baby-sit for Mary while she is at school and when she needs time on occasion to finish homework assignments.

Enter Noreen

Mary enrolls in classes and soon earns excellent grades. But those grades require sacrifice—John's not too happy about it all. What bothers him most is that Mary rarely seems in the mood to make love. John understands her dilemma. School consumes a lot of energy, and what is left must be devoted to housekeeping and caring for Tiffany. By bedtime Mary feels exhausted, and John realizes that to insist on making love under those conditions would be inconsiderate.

John makes the best of it with less frequent and more hurried lovemaking when he finds Mary in the mood, but he also misses the attention she used to give him and the tennis games they always played on Saturday mornings. Now Mary seldom spends time with him, much less plays tennis on Saturdays. Instead on the weekends she always does the housework and catches up on homework assigned for Monday classes.

John and Mary continue in this pattern for the next two years. Mary's account in John's Love Bank drops slowly but steadily. John begins wondering what happened to the lovely creature he married. She seems lost in her books, but ironically enough she doesn't want to discuss any of her classes with him.

"It's all stuff you had years ago," Mary tells him. "Besides, you're a math expert, and I'm not taking that much math."

Note that John's account in Mary's Love Bank holds steady, because John is helping to meet a very special need in her life right now—getting an education. Mary realizes they haven't spent much time together, but she deeply appreciates all John's sacrifices and his apparent total commitment to his family.

Things will be better as soon as I get my degree, she tells herself. So Mary plunges on into academia, not quite realizing how her husband feels.

Meanwhile at work John spends more and more time with an attractive product manager named Noreen. The company transfers her to his department, and they start working together on a regular basis. When Noreen's husband leaves her for another woman, John tries to give her as much comfort and support as he can. Over the months John's friendship with Noreen deepens daily, and she soon has a few hundred units deposited in John's Love Bank.

Noreen makes deposits when they talk together at coffee and at other opportune moments. John has no qualms about sharing the good and the bad experiences of his life with Noreen. Their conversations sometimes remind him of the "old days" with Mary.

So when John starts feeling frustrated due to Mary's lack of time for sex (or anything else but studying it seems) he shares his frustration with Noreen and finds her quite sympathetic. In fact Noreen lets John know that since her divorce she feels sexually frustrated, too.

The weeks and months fly by, and Mary finishes her bachelor's degree and launches into her master's program. "Only two more years and it's over," she tells John. "You've been wonderful to back me up like this."

John smiles and says he has been glad to do it, but inside he feels something else.

"She's just so wrapped up in that degree she can't think of anything else," John tells Noreen at coffee the next day. "I want her to have it, but I'm wondering if the price has been too much to pay."

A few weeks later, Mary is particularly overwhelmed with studying for mid-term exams. At the same time, John gets hit with a special project that forces him into a great deal of overtime, with Noreen helping him. One night as John and Noreen work late, alone, it happens. One moment John is telling Noreen about how lonely he feels. The next moment she is in his arms, and they are making love.

When it's over and they are getting ready to go home for the night, John is visibly agitated and guilt ridden. Noreen senses his feelings and tells him she doesn't want to wreck his marriage or come between him and Mary.

"Look," she says, "I have to be honest. I've fallen in love with you, and I want to make you happy. Why don't we just make love together when we can? That will be all I want."

On his way home John decides he doesn't feel so guilty after all. In fact, he starts feeling elated. Through no fault of her own, Mary is unable at present to meet his sexual needs. Now Noreen wants nothing more than to fill in as a temporary sexual partner. *Why not let her, since it is helping meet her needs, too?* John rationalizes. *It will all be temporary of course—until Mary is finished with school and can have more energy for sex.* Whatever guilt John feels he quickly quashes with a thought of his unfulfilled needs.

From that time on, John and Noreen make love at least once a week and sometimes more often. In less than a year, Noreen's account in John's Love Bank jumps to a thousand units, about the same as Mary's. Her huge increase occurs because she never does or says anything that makes John feel uncomfortable. Every sexual encounter is wildly passionate. In short, John thinks that Noreen is terrific, and he falls very much in love with her.

John's falling in love with Noreen does not mean he does not still love his wife. With no sexual frustrations, John's relationship to Mary improves a great deal. They include little Tiffany in everything they do together and make a special effort to enjoy family outings. When Mary has a brief break from studies and wants to make love, John is an enthusiastic partner. Those moments, unfortunately, do not happen very frequently.

Meanwhile John and Noreen work out their weekly rendezvous to a science. He never gives the right and wrong of the situation a second thought. That huge project John has taken on has continued to demand overtime, and Mary never suspects a thing.

In fact, Mary would have never known Noreen existed if it hadn't been for Jane, her good friend. Through another woman whose husband works in John's division, Jane hears about how cozy he and Noreen are at coffee breaks. She gets suspicious and does a bit of snooping. She discovers John and Noreen's affair and goes right to Mary with the news.

At first Mary does not believe Jane, but when she checks for herself she catches John red-handed—and red-faced.

John is shaken because he never believed he'd be discovered. If Mary had never known about Noreen, she could never have been hurt. For the first time, John feels deeply guilty. He begs Mary to forgive him and tries to explain why he did it.

"I could see how hard you were working with your studies, and I didn't want to be selfish and demand that we make love. The thing with Noreen just happened—then I guess I let it continue because I needed it. I never meant to hurt you. Now I can see that I was selfish after all and really stupid. I promise you it won't happen again."

Mary is heartbroken and furious. Why couldn't John have said something? Why did he have to betray their marriage in order to meet his needs? For the first time Mary sees that her drive for her degree has become a booby trap. She weeps uncontrollably, and John feels equally devastated. He begs Mary to forgive him and swears he will never see Noreen again.

Because she truly loves John, Mary forgives him and tries to make some changes. She cuts back on classes to make time for tennis again. She tries to make love to John several times a week, with passion and enthusiasm. John intends to be faithful, but in the first weeks after the confrontation he suffers the most severe depression of his life. You see, whether or not he likes it, his Love Bank has taken its deposits. He now loves Mary *and* Noreen. John misses Noreen, but he can't leave Mary. In short, John loves and needs both women. They both have substantial balances in his Love Bank, and he cannot seem to do without either one of them.

Hard as he tries, John cannot stay away from Noreen. To relieve his depression he gets back together with her and finds that she has also been depressed in his absence. She welcomes him back in a wild evening of lovemaking, and they plan more elaborate ways to get together without being discovered. But before long Mary becomes suspicious, and soon she knows she is sharing her husband with another woman, a woman to whom he has become addicted.

What Next?

At this point people like John and Mary often end up in my office. He wants to end the affair because of the growing pressure at home. She wants him to get rid of the other woman because it drives her crazy. Often the other woman has now grown tired of being noble and patient: She pressures the husband to divorce his wife and marry her.

The trouble is, the erring spouse—in this case the husband—can't bring himself to give up either woman. His lover provides some of his needs, and his wife provides others. He is like a donkey between two bales of hay, but instead of starving to death because he cannot decide which bale to choose, he tries to nibble on both bales!

Sometimes I am able to help and sometimes I am not. It all depends on whether or not the errant spouse and the lover can be separated permanently and whether or not the couple can learn to meet each other's basic marital needs.

What Ever Happened to Commitment?

Maybe you're still asking yourself, *Should I be concerned about my spouse having an affair if I don't meet her needs? Should my spouse fear that I might have an affair if my needs are not being met?* In reference to the needs described in this book, answer yes.

I realize this is not good news. "Whatever happened to commitment?" you may ask. "And what about *trust?* How can a marriage function if partners can't trust each other?"

I am all for commitment, and I agree that trust is a vital bonding link in any marriage. But twenty-five years of experience with thousands of people has taught me an undeniable truth: If any of a spouse's five basic emotional needs goes unmet, that spouse becomes vulnerable to the temptation of an affair. By examining each of these areas of need separately, spouses can learn how to take care of each other in ways that will make their marriages resistant to affairs. More important, their marriages can become far more exciting and fulfilling—and trusting—than ever before.

In the first chapter I described ten emotional needs of men and women. While all ten are shared by both sexes, five tend to be rated by women as most important, and the other five are rated by men as most important.

This disparity between men and women in regard to the priority of these ten needs makes it difficult for the two sexes to empathize with each other. "Why," each asks the other, "are these five things so important to you? None of them strikes me as so vital that I couldn't get along without them, at least for a while. What's the matter with you?"

Because of this lack of understanding, the couple unknowingly works at cross-purposes, each trying to fulfill the needs he or she feels, not the needs the mate feels. So wives often easily shower their husbands with affection because they appreciate it and want it so much themselves. Conversely, husbands smother their wives with sexual advances, because sex is one of their most pressing needs. Each becomes confused when at best that mate responds with mild pleasure and at worst becomes annoyed, irritated, or frigid.

This sort of behavior—in which one spouse gives the other something he or she really doesn't need that badly—becomes self-defeating and destructive. Because the priorities of men's needs are different than the priorities of women's needs, each partner must take the time to discover and recognize the other's most important needs: those with the highest priority. Amazingly, many people think they can do this simply through intuition, but I'm convinced it can only happen as a result of clear communication and effective training.

The husband and wife who commit themselves to meet each other's needs will lay a foundation for lifelong happiness in a marriage that is deeper and more satisfying than they ever dreamed possible.

In the next two chapters we will look at the most important need for most women (affection) and the most important need for most men (sex). We will start with the need for affection because when it's met, it lays the groundwork in meeting the need for sex.

In numerous counseling situations I have found men incredibly inept in regard to showing their wives affection. With few exceptions these men complain bitterly about "not enough sex." Meanwhile, their wives, who don't really understand how to have a fulfilling sexual relationship or how to enjoy making love, complain, "All he wants is my body; he never just wants to be affectionate." The frustration that results on both sides can easily lead to an affair and possible divorce. It need not be! Let me show you why.

3

AFFECTION

When Jane fell in love with Richard, she knew she had found her prince. At six feet three inches, Richard's 195 pounds were as lean and muscular at age twenty-three as they had been when Jane admired him on the basketball court in high school. Ruggedly handsome, Richard was the strong, silent type, which only made him more intriguing to Jane. Dates with Richard felt exciting, and when he held her in his arms the passion level went right off the scale.

"We've got the right chemistry," Jane assured herself.

However after just a few months of marriage, the passion began to pall. Jane started noticing something a bit odd: Whenever she cuddled up for a hug or a little kiss, Richard became sexually aroused almost immediately. Almost without exception physical contact led straight to the bedroom.

Jane also learned that Richard's "strong, silent" courting style had covered his tendencies for extreme moodiness and keeping almost everything to himself. Before they married, Richard had told Jane that his mother had died when he was just ten, and his father and two older brothers raised him. She hadn't thought too much of it. That's probably why he's so rugged and manly, she told herself.

Jane didn't realize that Richard had grown up in a home where displays of affection were not frequent before his mother died, and afterward they became almost nonexistent. He literally didn't know how to give affection, because he had received so little himself. For Richard affection in marriage was synonymous with sex, something that left Jane feeling disillusioned and used. As their marriage approached their first anniversary, Richard's account in Jane's Love Bank barely held its own.

At work, Jane was transferred to a new department, and there she met Bob, a warm and affable fellow who loved everyone. Bob had a habit of draping his arm over the shoulder of whomever he walked with—male and female alike. No one took offense. He was just a friendly man who liked everybody.

Jane noticed that she started to look forward to Bob's occasional hugs. They always made her feel good—warm and comfortable and cared for. One day they met in the hall.

"Hi, Jane, how ya doin'?" Bob greeted her as he gave her a little hug.

"You know, Bob," she said. "I've meant to tell you for a long time how much I appreciate your hugs. It's nice to meet a man who likes to do that."

"Well, then, come here!" he laughed and gave her another hug and a little kiss on the cheek.

Jane tried to act calm, but that little peck started her heart pounding. It continued pounding in the following weeks as she started receiving little notes from Bob. They were always tasteful and sweet. One said, "Good morning! Hope you have a great day! You're a fine person, and you deserve the best. Your friend, Bob."

Jane began to reciprocate with notes of her own. Before long she began to look forward to the arrival of Bob's latest note as the high point of her day. Sometimes he would bring her a little bouquet of flowers. That made her feel like a true princess.

They lunched together several times, and Bob's account in Jane's Love Bank climbed steadily. Jane found herself craving every expression of the gentle affection she received from Bob—the hugs, the smiles, the notes. Finally, she wrote a note to him: "I can't help it. I think I'm falling in love with you."

Bob didn't respond in kind but he continued to show Jane kindness and affection. The weeks went by, and one day they found themselves alone together in a secluded spot they had chosen for a hurried lunch-hour picnic. As they packed up to leave, Jane's hand touched Bob's, and she gave it a squeeze. Bob responded with an especially affectionate hug, and what followed came so naturally and beautifully Jane couldn't believe it. Making love with Bob was the most exciting experience of her life, because she knew he cared so much for her.

In the following weeks they slipped off together as often as possible for passionate lovemaking. Having sex with Bob was wonderful, because Jane could release all her emotions and become thoroughly involved. Bob's genuine affection made her feel loved and cared for as a person.

What had happened? Did Jane's wedding vows mean nothing to her? Was she just waiting for her chance to two-time her husband? Hardly. Jane simply felt so starved for affection that she was literally hugged into having an affair!

Affection Is the Cement of a Relationship

To most women affection symbolizes security, protection, comfort, and approval, vitally important commodities in their eyes. When a husband shows his wife affection, he sends the following messages:

- I'll take care of you and protect you. You are important to me, and I don't want anything to happen to you.
- I'm concerned about the problems you face, and I am with you.
- I think you've done a good job, and I'm so proud of you.

A hug can say any and all of the above. Men need to understand how strongly women need these affirmations. For the typical wife, there can hardly be enough of them.

I've mentioned hugging often because I believe it is a skill most men need to develop to show their wives affection. It is also a simple but effective way to build their accounts in a wife's Love Bank.

Most women love to hug. They hug each other, they hug children, animals, relatives—even stuffed animals. I'm not saying they will throw themselves into the arms of just anyone: They can get quite inhibited about hugging if they think it could be misinterpreted in a sexual way. But the rest of the time, across most countries and cultures, women hug and like to be hugged.

Obviously a man can display affection in other ways that can be equally important to a woman. A greeting card or a note expressing love and care can simply but effectively communicate the same emotions. Don't forget that all-time favorite—a bouquet of flowers. Women, almost universally, love to receive flowers. Occasionally I meet a man who likes to receive them, but most do not. For most women, however, flowers send a powerful message of love and concern.

An invitation to dinner also signals affection. It is a way of saying to one's wife, "You don't need to do what you ordinarily do for me. I'll treat you instead. You are special to me, and I want to show you how much I love and care for you."

Jokes abound on how, almost immediately after the wedding, a wife has to find her own way in and out of cars, houses, restaurants, and so on. But a sensitive husband will open the door for her at every opportunity—another way to tell her, "I love you and care about you."

Holding hands is a time-honored and effective sign of affection. Walks after dinner, back rubs, phone calls, and conversations with thoughtful and loving expressions all add units to the Love Bank. As more than one song has said, "There are a thousand ways to say I love you."

From a woman's point of view, affection is the essential cement of her relationship with a man. Without it, a woman probably feels alienated from her mate. With it she becomes tightly bonded to him while he adds units to his Love Bank account.

But She Knows I'm Not the Affectionate Type

Men must get through their heads this vital idea: Women find affection important in its own right. They love the feeling that accompanies both the bestowal and the reception of affection, but it has nothing to do with sex. Most of the affection they give and receive is not intended to be sexual. You might better compare it to the emotion they exchange with their children or pets.

All of this confuses the typical male. He sees showing affection as part of sexual foreplay, and he is normally aroused in a flash. In other cases men simply want to skip the affection business; they are aroused already.

Let's look in on a hypothetical couple we'll call Brenda and Bruce. They have been having tension lately because Brenda hasn't responded with much enthusiasm to Bruce's requests for sex. As our scene opens she senses Bruce has that look in his eye again, and she tries to head him off at the pass: "Bruce, let's just relax for a few minutes. Then maybe you can hold my hand, and we can hug. I'm not ready for sex just like that. I need a little affection first."

Bruce bristles with a bit of macho impatience and says, "You've known me for years. I'm not the affectionate type, and I'm not going to start now!"

Does this sound incredible or farfetched? I hear versions of it regularly in my office. Bruce fails to see the irony in wanting sex but refusing to give his wife affection. A man who growls, "I'm not the affectionate type," while reaching for his wife's body to satisfy his desires for sex, is like a salesman who tries to close a deal by saying, "I'm not the friendly type—sign here, you turkey. I've got another appointment waiting."

Although they shouldn't have a hard time understanding this simple logic, men lose track of Harley's First Law of Marriage:

> When it comes to sex and affection,
> you can't have one without the other.

Any Man Can Learn to Be Affectionate

Affection is so important for women that they become confused when their husbands don't respond in kind. For example, a wife may call her husband at work, just to talk. She would love to receive such a call and is sure he feels the same. She often feels disappointed when he cuts it short because, "I've got all this stuff to finish by five o'clock." It doesn't mean the husband doesn't love her; he simply has different priorities because of a different set of basic needs.

When I go on a trip, I often find little notes Joyce has packed among my clothes. She is telling me she loves me, of course, but the notes send another message as well. Joyce would like to get the same little notes from me, and I have tried to leave such notes behind—on her pillow, for example—when I go out of town.

My needs for protection, approval, and care are not the same as hers, nor are they met in similar ways. I've had to discover these differences and act accordingly. For example, when we walk through a shopping center, it is important to her that we hold hands, something that would not occur to me naturally or automatically. She has encouraged me to take her hand, and I'm glad to do so, because I know she enjoys that and it says something she wants to hear.

When I try to explain this kind of hand holding to some husbands in my counseling office, they may question my manhood a bit. Isn't my wife "leading me by the nose" so to speak? I reply that in my opinion nothing could be further from the truth. If holding Joyce's hand in a shopping center makes her feel loved and cherished, I would be a fool to refuse to do it. I appreciate her coaching on how to show affection. I promised to care for her when I married her, and I meant every word of it. If she explains how I can best give her the care she wants, I'm willing to learn, because I want her happiness.

Almost all men need some instruction in how to become more affectionate, and those who have developed such loving habits have usually learned how to do so from good coaches—perhaps former girlfriends. In most marriages, a man's wife can become his best teacher, if he approaches her for help in the right way.

First, you need to explain to her that you love her very much, but often fail to express your deep love and care for her appropriately. Then you should ask her to help you learn to express this affection, which you already feel, in ways she will appreciate.

Initially she will probably feel puzzled by such a request. "When you love someone, affection comes naturally!" she may reply. She may not realize that affection comes more naturally for her than it does for you.

She may think that you have sex on your mind and have devised some new angle to improve your sexual relationship.

"I don't think I let you know how much I really care for you," you may answer. "I just assume you know, because I go to work, take you out, and help you around the house. I should be doing more to tell you how much I care about you."

"Sounds great! When do we start?"

She can help you by making a list of those signs of care that mean the most to her. Women usually express a need for physical closeness, such as hugging, hand holding, and sitting close together. Kissing is very important to most women, as are token gifts and cards that express your emotional attachment and commitment. Women love to have their husbands take them out to dinner, and usually a wife regards any effort her husband makes to join her in shopping for food and clothing as a sign of affection. When I counsel women who've expressed a need for affection, I use a form, Affection Inventory, to help them identify acts of affection that are most important to them.

Here are a few habits that go a long way toward helping you become an affectionate husband:

- Hug and kiss your wife every morning while you are still in bed.
- Tell her that you love her while you're having breakfast together.
- Kiss her before you leave for work.
- Call her during the day to see how she is doing.
- Bring her flowers once in a while as a surprise (be sure to include a card that expresses your love for her).
- Gifts for special occasions (birthday, anniversary, Christmas, Mother's Day, and Valentine's Day) should be sentimental, not practical. Learn how to shop for a woman.
- After work, call her before you leave for home, so that she can know when to expect you.
- When you arrive home from work, give her a hug and kiss and spend a few minutes talking to her about how her day went.
- Help with the dishes, after dinner.
- Hug and kiss her every night, before you both go to sleep.

Once your wife has helped you identify habits that will meet her need for affection, create a plan that sees to it that you'll learn those habits. To repeat a point I make throughout this book, knowing what your spouse needs does not meet the need. You must learn new habits that transform that knowledge into action. Then and only then is that need met. Don't build up your wife's hopes with your good intentions. Go one step further: Learn the habits of affection. If you know your wife's needs and then fail to deliver, your relationship will be worse than it was before you gained understanding. At least then you could plead ignorance!

Your plan to learn habits of affection should be carefully written down so that you'll be more likely to stay on course. Clients I counsel use a form, Strategy to Meet the Need of Affection, to describe their plan. The form simply requires couples to identify the habits they wish to learn and describe how they plan to learn them.

Habits usually take time to develop—sometimes weeks, sometimes months. Your plan should include the time you expect to be "in training." The easiest habits to learn are those that you enjoy performing, the most difficult are the ones you tend to find uncomfortable. At first, most changes of behavior seem and look awkward. It's not spontaneous and smooth; it's contrived. This is especially true for many habits of affection. For that reason, many too quickly give up trying to develop these habits. But you'll find that after a behavior has been repeated a number of times, it becomes more natural and spontaneous. What begins as uncomfortable can become second nature to you.

Another obstacle is that habits of affection are not necessarily motivated by your own need; they are motivated by your desire to meet your wife's need. She may be offended at first when you're not as interested in affection as she is. But eventually, you will find yourself enjoying your time of affection together, and when that happens she won't be concerned about how it developed. You'll both be winners: She will have what she needs from the man who enjoys meeting the need.

Sex Begins with Affection

Over the years I have seen nothing more devastating to a marriage than an affair. Sadly enough, most affairs start because of a lack of affection (for the wife) and lack of sex (for the husband). It's quite a vicious cycle. She doesn't get enough affection, so she shuts him off sexually. He doesn't get enough sex, so the last thing he feels like being is affectionate.

The solution to this tragic cycle is for someone to break it. I made my reputation as a marriage counselor convincing wives that if they met their husbands' sexual need, their husbands would be willing to meet their need for affection in return, and any other needs, for that matter. It worked so well that I built a thriving practice overnight, so to speak.

But it can also be done the other way around, having a husband meet his wife's need for affection first. I've discovered that when her need is met, she's usually much more willing to meet his need for sex. Since I begin this book with the wife's need for affection, I recommend that if your need for sex is not being fulfilled, take the initiative by learning to meet your wife's need for affection first.

Affection is the environment of the marriage while sex is an *event*. Affection is a way of life, a canopy that covers and protects a marriage. It's a direct and convincing expression of love that gives the event of sex a more appropriate context. Most women need affection before sex means much to them.

Because men tend to translate affection into sex so readily, I put emphasis on learning sexless affection. I try to teach a husband to make affection a nonsexual way of relating to his spouse. He learns not to just turn it on and off to get some sex. Whenever he and his spouse come together, a big hug and kiss should be routine. In fact, almost every interaction between them should include affectionate words and gestures. I believe every marriage should have an atmosphere that says, "I really love you and I know you love me."

When I talk about sexless affection, many men become confused. What is he supposed to do with his natural feeling of sexual arousal, which can be triggered by almost any act of affection? He wants to know if he has to "take cold showers" to keep cool. I point out to him that when he was dating, he was just as sexually aroused as he is now, even more so! But he showed plenty of affection and attention that did not include groping and grabbing. He treated the young lady with respect and tenderness.

Many husbands remember the passionate encounters of their courting days and want to know, "Why doesn't she get turned on the way she did before we were married?"

44

I patiently explain that he isn't treating her the way he did back then. After marriage he thought he could do away with the preliminaries and get right to the main event. But it turns out that the "preliminaries" are not only required for a fulfilling sexual relationship, they're also needed in their own right. In many cases what he thinks are preliminaries are her "main event."

In most cases, a woman needs to feel a oneness with her husband before she has sex with him. A couple achieves this feeling through the exchange of affection and undivided attention.

Her need for this one-spirit unity helps us understand how affairs develop. In the typical affair, a woman has sex with a man after he has demonstrated his love for her by showering her with affection. Because her lover has expressed such care for her, the physical union is usually characterized by a degree of ecstacy otherwise unknown to her in marriage. She concludes that her lover is right for her because she doesn't feel the same way when she makes love to her husband.

In truth, any marriage can have the sizzle of an affair if it has that strong one-spirit bond. It's a tragic misperception for her to think that her husband is not right for her based on a comparison of feelings at a moment in time. If he were to lay the groundwork with affection, their bond would be restored and the affair would be seen for what it really is: a misguided effort to have an important emotional need met.

When your marriage is struggling sexually, look for the missing element of affection. Without the environment, the sexual event is contrived and unnatural for many women. All too often she reluctantly agrees to have sex with her husband, even though she knows she won't enjoy it. In an affair, the conditions that guarantee fulfilling sex—the bonding that comes with affection—are met. Her lover has taken time and action to create the right environment for sex. Consequently, she feels sexually aroused at the very thought of him.

Most of the women I've counseled crave affection. I try to help their husbands understand the pleasure women feel when this need is met. Although they're not the same as those experienced during sex, they form a vital part of a romantic relationship. Without it, a woman's sexual experience is incomplete.

Many husbands have this all backwards. For them, sexual arousal makes them feel more affectionate. They try to explain to their wives the importance of having sex more often so that they'll feel like being affectionate. But that argument usually falls on deaf ears. Some women will have sex with their husbands just for the affection they receive while making love, but it tends to leave them resentful and bitter. As soon as sex is over, their husbands go back to their unaffectionate ways, leaving their wives feeling unloved. They feel that all their husbands want is sex, and they don't really care about them in any other way. That attitude destroys their feeling of intimacy and the bond of unity. But that attitude can change if their husbands learn to create an environment of affection by learning habits that produce a steady stream of love and care.

Just as men want their wives' sexual response to be spontaneous, women prefer their husbands' affection to be spontaneous. There is a certain spontaneity to our behavior once it's well learned, but when we try to develop new behavior it seems contrived and unnatural. At first, efforts to be affectionate may not be very convincing and, as a result, may not have the effect of spontaneous affection. But with practice, the affectionate behavior eventually conveys accurately the feeling of care that husbands have for their wives. That, in turn, creates the environment necessary for a more spontaneous sexual response in a woman.

A woman's need for affection is probably her deepest emotional need. But all that I've said here will prove of little value if a wife fails to understand that her husband has an equally deep need for sex. In the next chapter I'll confront the woman in an effort to explain why, for men, sex is not just one of several ways to end a lovely evening. To the typical man, sex is like air or water. He can't do without it very well.

If a wife fails to understand the power of the male sex appetite, she will wind up having a husband who's tense and frustrated at best. At worst, someone else may step forward to meet his need and, tragically enough, that happens all too often in our society. But it can all be avoided if husbands learn to be more affectionate and wives respond with more eagerness to make love. As Harley's First Law of Marriage says:

> When it comes to sex
> and affection, you can't have one
> without the other.

Questions for Him

1. On a scale of one to ten, with ten being "very affectionate," how affectionate am I toward my wife? How would she rate me?
2. Is affection the environment for our entire marriage?
3. In the past have I tended to equate affection with getting sexually aroused? Why hasn't this worked?
4. In what specific ways do I show my wife affection?
5. Would I be willing to have her coach me in how to show her more affection in the ways she really likes it?

Questions for Her

1. Is affection as important to me as this chapter claims?
2. If I'm not getting enough affection from my husband, am I willing to put aside my pride and patiently coach him?
3. Would I find it easier to make love if I felt he were truly interested in me and affectionate toward me?

To Consider Together

1. Do we need to talk about affection? If so, what exactly do we need to share?
2. Is there enough affection in our marriage? What examples can we give?
3. How can we have "affection practice"? What is comfortable for both of us?

4

THE FIRST THING
HE CAN'T DO WITHOUT

SEXUAL FULFILLMENT

"Before we married, Jim was so romantic and affectionate—a regular Don Juan. Now he seems more like Attila the Hun."

"When John wants sex, he wants it right now. He doesn't care how I feel; all he cares about is satisfying himself."

"Bob has turned into an animal. All he can ever think about is sex, sex, sex!"

When I hear wives make remarks like these in my counseling office, I understand how disillusioned they must feel. At one time men who knew how to give them affection swept these women off their feet. But once committed in marriage, all that affection vaporized, and what was left seemed like pure lust. Was the affection during courtship simply a ploy to captivate a woman for sexual gratification?

"Why do you think your husband acts the way he does?" I ask.

"Because he is inconsiderate," is the usual answer—or words to that effect.

These women share a real and very widespread problem. I describe it simply in Harley's First Corollary:

> The typical wife doesn't understand her husband's deep need for sex any more than the typical husband understands his wife's deep need for affection.

If both sides want to listen and change, a couple may solve this without much difficulty. In chapter 3, I was fairly hard on the men, because I wholeheartedly believe that their inability to show affection is such a crucial problem. Remember, *affection is the environment of the marriage, sex is the special event.*

At the same time it does wonders for a wife to grasp just how special a man finds sex. He isn't "pawing and grabbing" at her because he has turned into a lusting monster. He is pawing and grabbing because he needs something—very badly. Many men tell me they wish their sex drive weren't so strong. As one thirty-two-year-old executive put it, "I feel like a fool—like I'm begging her or even raping her, but I can't help it. I *need* to make love!"

Why Men Often Wind Up Feeling Cheated

When a man chooses a wife, he promises to remain faithful to her for life. This means that he believes his wife will be his only sexual partner "until death do us part." He makes this commitment because he trusts her to be as sexually interested in him as he is in her. He trusts her to be sexually available to him whenever he needs to make love and to meet all his sexual needs, just as she trusts him to meet her emotional needs.

Unfortunately in many marriages the man finds that putting his trust in this woman has turned into one of the biggest mistakes of his life. He has agreed to limit his sexual experience to a wife who is unwilling to meet that vital need. He finds himself up the proverbial creek without a paddle. If his religious or moral convictions are strong, he may try to make the best of it. Some husbands tough it out, but many cannot. They find sex elsewhere.

The unfaithful man justifies it in terms of his wife's failure to keep her sexual commitment to him. When she discovers his unfaithfulness, she may try to "correct her error" and improve their sexual relationship, but by then it's often too late. She feels hurt and resentful, and he has become deeply involved in an affair.

One of the strangest studies in human behavior is the married man who is sexually attracted to another woman. He often seems possessed. I have known bank presidents, successful politicians, pastors of flourishing churches, leaders in every walk of life who have thrown away careers and let their life achievements go down the drain for a special sexual relationship. They explain to me in no uncertain terms that without this relationship everything else in life seems meaningless to them.

I sit and listen to these pathetic and bewildered men so motivated by their need for sex that their reasoning capacities have turned to mush. Ordinarily I would tend to admire these intelligent, successful, and otherwise responsible individuals. But their misdirected sex drive has them completely unraveled.

While this sequence of events is an insane way to live, my counseling experience leads me to believe that as many as half of all married couples go through the agony of unfaithfulness and affairs. I believe that in most marriages a couple may easily prevent this tragedy. Prevention begins with an understanding of the differences between the sexuality of men and women.

What's the Difference?

How different are men and women in regard to sexual drive and awareness of their sexuality?

Over the years, I have collected over 40,000 questionnaires from clients, which ask about their sexual history and sexual behavior. From the results of these questionnaires, it is apparent that almost all men masturbate, and many start at a very young age (eight to ten). On the other hand, girls who masturbate begin much later, most often in late teens and early twenties, and over half the women we surveyed had never masturbated at all.

The first heterosexual experiences reported by the men and women we surveyed took place at essentially the same ages (between thirteen and sixteen). But their reports of that experience differed remarkably. Almost every man surveyed enjoyed his first heterosexual encounter, while most women reported finding it a disappointment.

I believe at least part of this discrepancy lies in the reasons boys and girls engage in sex. For the most part boys are motivated by a strong sex drive and a history of sexual responsiveness through masturbation, while girls do not come to that first encounter with much of a sexual history at all. Many do not know what to expect. A desire to be liked by their boyfriend, or curiosity—"What *is* the big deal about sex, anyway?" they ask—motivates them, but not the feeling of an urgent need for sexual gratification.

This disparity in terms of sexual need and experience lies at the root of many marital problems, even in this day of supposed sexual liberation and enlightenment. Young men and women come together in marriage from opposite ends of the pole: He is more sexually experienced and motivated by strong desires; she is less (often much less) experienced, less motivated, and sometimes naive. Furthermore, his experience is so visceral and almost automatic that he usually does not understand that most women must learn how to respond sexually, and he is not prepared to teach his bride how to enjoy her own sexuality. He just knows how much he loves it and assumes that what he enjoys must feel at least as good to her. Most young husbands discover the falsehood of that assumption before very long; they learn instead the frustrating truth that the wonderful sexual discoveries they have made seem much less meaningful to their brides. For many men this becomes a source of unparalleled frustration.

Entering Marriage Sexually Unprepared

Although great strides have been made in the last thirty years in the area of premarital sexual counseling and in the development of helpful literature for newly married couples, many men and women still enter marriage sexually unprepared. Men, of course, feel they are *very* prepared, but *being ready for sex and being prepared to make love are two different things.*

Men experience sexual arousal and climax with relative ease. Precisely the opposite is true for the majority of women. Reports of heavy teenage sexual activity notwithstanding, my counseling experience has shown me that even sexually active women usually enter marriage having rarely experienced arousal or climax. Many of these women have *never* experienced a climax prior to marriage.

Husbands often enter marriage assuming their wives have far more sexual sophistication than they have. Because they don't want to appear naive or lacking in sexual prowess, some wives don't level with their husbands. Instead they act as though they truly experience sexual arousal and a climax when in fact they do not. Others endure sex as a duty. Many wives find sex with their husbands a catastrophic experience because they do not understand their own sexuality well enough to help their husbands make an appropriate sexual adjustment to them. Many otherwise compatible couples fail to find sexual fulfillment due to their own ignorance and deception.

As the bottom line many husbands do without sex or exist on a very limited diet (in their opinion). The husband blames the wife, of course, but the real culprit is sexual incompatibility, which needs to be overcome through the efforts of *both* partners, not just the woman.

A man cannot achieve sexual fulfillment in his marriage unless his wife is sexually fulfilled as well. While I have maintained that men need sex more than women, unless a woman joins her husband in the sexual experience, his need for sex remains unmet. Therefore a woman does her husband no favors by sacrificing her body to his sexual advances. He can feel sexually satisfied only when she joins him in the experience of lovemaking.

Since men and women differ so greatly in the way they come to enjoy sex, no wonder we find so much sexual incompatibility in marriage. The key of communication unlocks the doors of ignorance and opens up to each couple the opportunity for sexual compatibility. In the remaining pages of this chapter I will outline some of the most important points men and women need to communicate to each other to achieve sexual compatibility.

How to Achieve Sexual Compatibility

Achieving sexual compatibility involves two important steps:

1. *Overcome your sexual ignorance.* A husband and wife must each understand their own sexuality and their own sexual responses.
2. *Communicate your sexual understanding to each other.* A husband and wife must learn how to share what they have learned about their own sexual responses, so that they can each achieve sexual pleasure and fulfillment together.

To help you develop sexual compatibility in your marriage, the rest of this chapter will present a quick lesson in human sexuality. While some of this material may seem a bit unromantic and clinical, bear with me. The better you understand the following information, the better you can meet each other's needs sexually.

Many sexual conflicts are resolved when a husband and wife learn what actually happens—emotionally and physiologically—when they make love to each other.

The sexual experience divides into four stages: *arousal, plateau, climax,* and *recovery.*

During *arousal* the man and woman begin to sense sexual feelings. His penis usually becomes erect, and her vagina usually begins to lubricate. If a man's penis and a woman's clitoris are stimulated properly, they pass into the *plateau* stage. In this stage his penis becomes very hard and her vagina contracts, providing greater resistance and a heightened sensation during intercourse. The *climax,* which lasts only a few seconds, is the peak of the sexual experience. At this time the penis ejects semen in bursts (ejaculation), and the vagina alternately contracts and releases several times. The *recovery* period follows, in which both partners feel peaceful and relaxed; the penis becomes soft, and the vagina, no longer secreting lubricating fluid, relaxes.

While men and women experience the same four stages, they do not do so in the same physical and emotional ways. What works for a man does not work for a woman, and conversely, what works for a woman does not work for a man. Couples who wish to experience sexual compatibility need to appreciate and understand the differences.

We will discuss each stage of the sexual response separately and show some of the most important differences.

Arousal: How It All Starts

In the earliest stages of lovemaking one can already see the differences between a man and woman by the ways they become excited and the manner in which each responds.

Most men can become aroused in a variety of ways, but the hands-down favorite is by visual means. Numerous magazines, calendars, films, videocassettes, and so on that feature nude or barely clad women all cash in on one thing: Men like to look at naked women. During counseling sessions, wives readily testify that their husbands enjoy watching them undress and that, when they are seen naked, arousal follows in just a few seconds.

A man easily experiences arousal, which may happen several times a day. Many nonvisual and visual experiences can do it: a scent of perfume in an elevator, watching a woman's walk, looking at a photo of a scantily clad woman, or even daydreaming.

Wives sometimes express dismay at their husbands' ability to be sexually aroused by other women, but they need to understand that their husbands are not being promiscuous or unfaithful. They have simply experienced a characteristic male reaction. Arousal in itself doesn't mean that much to a man: It may occur relatively effortlessly, and he sometimes experiences it whether or not he wants to.

Women may find this hard to understand, because they experience arousal so differently from the way men do. Much more complicated and deliberate, the woman's excitement does not, in most cases, depend on visual stimulation. Although male centerfolds in women's magazines get a lot of attention, most women really think of them more as humorous conversation pieces than a means of genuine sexual stimulation.

For the average woman, getting aroused is more a matter of mind-set than the result of any stimulation, visual or otherwise. A woman can choose whether or not she wants to experience arousal, depending on her emotional attachment to a particular man. Qualities like affection, attentiveness, warmth of personality, kindness, and tender sensitivity do more to arouse her than any special technique a man may have developed. A man with the qualities mentioned above makes a woman feel that he understands her and has chosen to care for her.

A woman looks for all these signs in the eyes of a man. Perhaps this is why, when asked what they first notice about a man, many females will say, "His eyes." One wife described the special appreciation her husband had of her as his ability to "be aware of me as a person," not just a sex partner. The caring he showed by looking at her as if she was special meant a lot to their relationship. In our society we make much of the idea of handsome men getting together with beautiful women, but for many women a man's looks are not the most critical issue. A tender touch and gentle treatment may mean more than a handsome face or trim physique.

A man can do much to arouse or suppress his wife's sexual feelings by the way he touches her. His embrace, his kiss, and his caress must convey tender attentiveness and special caring. Feelings of affection and care give you the keys to a woman's arousal.

If a woman feels convinced that her husband possesses these warm and affectionate qualities, she can *decide* to engage in a process that leads to sexual arousal. In most extramarital affairs, the woman finds her lover irresistible because he shows her the tenderness and kindness she has not found with her spouse. The common scenario in an affair sees the man being overwhelmed by the woman's passionate pursuit and vigorous sexual aggressiveness. In most cases the woman responds to the fantasy of her ideal man, embodied in her lover. It doesn't matter if the man is a good guy or a rat. What really matters is how she perceives him—the aura he created by affectionate and thoughtful actions.

Once a woman decides to be aroused, she's ready to receive and respond to appropriate tactile stimulation, such as the caressing of her body (especially the breasts and nipples) and stimulation of the area surrounding the clitoris. The very same stimulation, given to an unreceptive woman, does not arouse her sexually at all. It becomes a source of great irritation to the woman who has not chosen to be aroused. When intercourse begins, a woman needs to sustain strong stimulation to her clitoris and vaginal opening. A woman learns to create this more intensive stimulation by (1) contracting her pubococcygeus (PCG) muscle, which tightens the vagina on the inserted penis; (2) thrusting her pelvis rapidly; (3) and assuming a position that increases pressure on the clitoris and resistance to the penis in the vaginal opening.

A few minutes of this physical stimulation usually brings an aroused woman (and her aroused husband) to the next stage—the sexual plateau.

Plateau: The Best Stage of Lovemaking

While women need very special and intense stimulation to reach a plateau, men need much less stimulation. Intercourse itself is almost always sufficient for men, and many reach a plateau with even less stimulation.

Unfortunately her need for more stimulation and his need for less creates a common sexual problem: premature ejaculation—which means that he comes to a climax too soon. As she thrusts quickly to stimulate herself to the plateau, the stimulation becomes too great for him. He experiences a climax and loses his erection before she can reach a plateau or climax.

On the other hand, if a man tries to hold back a climax, he may find himself falling from the plateau stage, back to arousal, and his penis softens. Although he may continue intercourse, his penis is not hard enough to give his wife the stimulation she needs.

For many men, maintaining the plateau stage without rising to a climax or receding to arousal is a challenge. When having intercourse, the man must hold the plateau about ten minutes, the time his wife needs to reach the plateau. Then she may need another five minutes to experience a climax. Men commonly climax before their wives have enough stimulation to enjoy the plateau or reach climax. Even the best intentioned man needs training to achieve this goal.

The Climax: Ecstasy or Anxiety?

In recent years many books and articles have extolled the climax (or orgasm) as an ecstatic experience that both partners should try to reach simultaneously for optimal pleasure. Because of all this publicity, the climax has become distorted and some couples have lost sight of the entire lovemaking experience, in an effort to reach their goal of achieving climax. When a couple feels anxiety rather than an enjoyment of each other, they are putting too much importance on performance and not enough on enjoying each other in their lovemaking.

The woman who knows how to reach a plateau is only one small step away from reaching a climax; it only takes more time and stimulation. However some women I've counseled have confided in me that they really don't find reaching climax worth the effort it takes to do so. They have reached it at times, but they are quite happy with the sex act without an orgasm and wish their husbands would not frequently pressure them to climax. I generally encourage men to let their wives decide whether or not to experience climax.

In my practice I have observed that women with an abundance of energy usually choose to climax whenever they make love. Women with less energy or women who feel tired after a long, hard day often choose not to climax. Men, on the other hand, whether full of energy or exhausted, almost always choose to climax, because it requires such little additional effort.

A good sexual relationship takes this difference of effort into account. A sensitive man will not put pressure on his wife to climax, because he realizes she may enjoy sex more without one. Anxiety over whether or not to climax has no place in a fulfilling sexual relationship.

If you have never reached a climax or have difficulty, especially during intercourse, I suggest a book by Georgia Kline-Graber, R.N., and Benjamin Graber, M.D.: *Women's Orgasm: A Guide to Sexual Satisfaction* (New York: Warner Books, 1975). This book is particularly useful to women who do not know how to climax because of the way it takes the reader through the process, clearly and step by step. The chapter entitled "A Ten-Step Program for Achieving Orgasm with Intercourse" is excellent, especially for women who know how to climax, but not during intercourse. I found that not all of the recommended steps are necessary to achieve a successful outcome. You may modify them to accommodate your values and sensitivities. Call 1-800-343-9204 (Little Brown order department) to order the book.

Recovery: Afterglow or Resentment?

An appropriate description of the recovery phase is an "afterglow," with both partners lying in each other's arms, feeling completely fulfilled. But because men and women do not share the same instincts after a climax, this ideal state eludes many couples.

Characteristically, following a climax, a woman falls back into the plateau stage and can reach another climax, if she so chooses. If she does not decide to climax again, she slowly falls back to arousal and then finally to an unaroused level. As this takes place she feels a deep sense of peace come over her and generally has a deep desire for some affection. Many women I counsel report that this feeling may remain for up to an hour after intercourse.

During the recovery period, men do not experience the same feelings. A second climax for men is not as desirable because it requires much more effort than the first, if a man can achieve it at all. For most men a third climax within a short period of time is nearly impossible. Unlike the woman, the man does not fall back to the plateau after climax—he usually falls back into arousal, and even that occurs only momentarily. Many men find themselves totally uninterested in sex within a minute of a climax. Often such men will jump up and take a shower or roll over and go to sleep. Many a honeymoon has been destroyed by such insensitive behavior.

Each couple must work out for themselves a proper sense of timing at the recovery stage. A man should be ready to bring his wife to another sexual climax through digital stimulation if she chooses, or he should continue showing her affection for at least fifteen to twenty minutes. Don't let this warm and meaningful time for conversation escape you.

On the other hand, a woman must not take her husband's sudden loss of sexual interest as a rejection of her. She needs to understand that the purely physical part of his sex drive rises after a period of physical abstinence and falls shortly after a climax. This does not mean that he no longer loves her, despite the fact that his sex drive has momentarily hit a low point.

Solving Sexual Problems

While sexual problems cause tension and unhappiness in many marriages, these difficulties can be solved more easily than one might think. In most cases it merely requires education. To deal with such problems, the couple willing to learn what they need to know and to practice it together will achieve fulfillment. Wives especially need to learn more about their sexuality. Before they can meet their husband's need for sex, they must know how to experience each of the stages I have described.

Many ask me, "How do we get educated?" It depends on how serious a problem you face. You may solve it by reading together any number of excellent books that discuss and illustrate sex for the married couple. Because it falls beyond the scope of this book, I have not attempted to go into detail on how to develop skills in lovemaking.

Read any sex manual with the goal of finding out what works for the two of you. Many such books will bombard you with all kinds of sexual procedures. But remember that some will work; some won't. No two couples respond in exactly the same manner. You must reach no "standard" other than feeling fulfilled, satisfied, and loved.

If you have a major sexual problem, you may need to visit a trained sex therapist. I have used sex therapy to help guide a few clients with sexual problems. But because each case I handle is of such an individual nature, I have not discussed therapeutic procedure here. If you feel your problem needs the individual attention of a sex therapist, it would be wise for you to read the books I have recommended first. Then you can more intelligently explain your problems and identify a counselor who has the proper credentials to help you solve the problem.

One of the tragic ironies of my job appears when I counsel couples in their seventies for sexual incompatibility. Almost always they resolve their problem within a few weeks, and many experience sexual fulfillment for the first time after forty or fifty years of marriage. "What a difference this would have made in our marriage," they often report. While I am happy that they finally resolved a longstanding and frustrating marital problem, I feel sad for the years they unnecessarily endured the guilt, anger, and depression that often accompany sexual incompatibility.

Meeting Each Other's Needs

As I said in chapter 1, I want to make husbands and wives aware of each other's five most important emotional needs and how to meet them. I have started the discussion of these basic needs with the ones I believe are absolutely foundational to a good marriage: affection for her and sex for him.

You may have found some of what I've said in this chapter irritating or even disgusting. Perhaps I offended some wives by talking about their need to "learn" about their sexuality. I'm willing to take that risk, because the stakes are so high. As I counsel couple after couple, two basic problems surface repeatedly. You may think of them as embarrassing, galling, or infuriating, but here are the facts:

1. While usually more in touch with their own sexuality because it is such a basic male drive, many men lack skill in lovemaking because they fail to understand a woman's need for affection as part of the sexual process. When a man learns to be affectionate, his lovemaking will become very different. The man interested only in satisfying his hunger for sex molests his wife more than anything else, because his technique is insensitive to her feelings. He uses his wife's body for his own pleasure while she gets more and more infuriated.
2. Conversely, many women don't understand their own sexuality well enough to know how to enjoy meeting a husband's compelling need for sex. In order to satisfy her husband sexually a wife must also feel satisfied. I try to encourage wives not to simply make their bodies available on a more regular basis; rather they should commit themselves to learning to enjoy the sex relationship as much as their husbands do.

The Marital Golden Rule

Obviously, for the wife to enjoy sex she will need help from her husband. If he does not give her the affection and tenderness she needs, she will feel that he is insensitive and uncaring. This principle of reciprocity is applied throughout this book. You can't enjoy your end of a marriage if your spouse doesn't enjoy his or her end. If you care about your spouse, you don't use or deny your spouse out of selfishness or ignorance.

Almost all cultures and ages know the Golden Rule. Jesus Christ taught us: "Do to others as you would have them do to you" (Luke 6:31). As you think about the concepts presented so far and look ahead to the other eight needs, please consider this slight revision of the Golden Rule. I call it Harley's Second Law of Marriage:

> Meet your spouse's needs
> as you would want your spouse
> to meet yours.

Questions for Her

1. On a scale of one to ten, with ten being "very satisfactory," how would you rate the four stages of your sexual response with your husband?

   Arousal_____ Plateau_____ Climax_____ Recovery_____

2. If you rated any of the four steps fairly low, what do you think is the problem? Does it lie with him or you or both of you?

3. After reading this chapter, what did you learn about your husband's need for sex?

Questions for Him

1. If your wife commented on your sexual desires and technique to a sex therapist, what do you think she would say?

2. How would you describe your sexual diet?

   Steady_____ Spasmodic_____ Starvation_____

3. According to the author, a woman is aroused by her husband's affection, attentiveness, warmth, kindness, and tender sensitivity. Are these qualities you consistently try to develop and express? What do you think your wife would say in answer to this question?

To Consider Together

1. Are we both having a satisfactory sexual experience? If not, at what stages are we having problems, and how can we change that?

2. Do we need to study a good sex manual together?

3. In the areas of affection and sex, are we practicing the author's version of the Golden Rule: "Meet your spouse's needs as you would want your spouse to meet yours"?

5

SHE NEEDS HIM TO TALK TO HER

CONVERSATION

When Jill and Harry dated, it was just one long conversation. On days when they could not be together in person, they often talked on the phone, sometimes for an hour or more. They rarely planned formal dates, because their real interest lay in seeing and talking with each other. Sometimes they got so busy talking they forgot to do whatever they had planned for the evening.

After their marriage, Jill and Harry found their conversations declining sharply. Both became involved in other things that took up more of their time. When they did have an opportunity to sit down and talk, Jill discovered Harry had less and less to say. When he came home from work, he generally buried his head in the newspaper, watched television, and went to bed early. It did not mean that Harry was uninterested in Jill or depressed about anything. He simply wanted to relax after a hard day at the office.

"Honey," Jill said one day, "I really miss our talks. I wish we could talk more the way we used to."

"Yeah," Harry replied, "I enjoyed those times, too. What would you like to talk about?"

That comment did not score as a deposit in Jill's Love Bank. She didn't say it, but she thought, *If you don't know the answer to that question, then I guess we don't have anything to talk about.*

After that Jill began to wonder why things had changed. Harry could still be talkative when he wanted to—for example, with a group of people at a ball game. He seemed to reserve his silence for her alone, and she found it hard not to resent it.

Harry and Jill frequently spent time with Tom and Kay, a couple their same age in the neighborhood. Tom, Jill noticed, seemed to make a practice of directing his conversation to her. He seemed not to have any problem thinking of things to talk about.

Over a period of time, Jill found that getting together with Tom and Kay had become a high point of her week. She looked forward to those times when she could talk about the various things on her mind. Tom always listened attentively and did a great job of holding up his half of the conversation. Whenever they found themselves in large groups— at parties for example—Tom would pick her out to be with and talk to. He would sit with Jill at meetings and invite her to special events they found mutually interesting. They became good friends. Of course Tom accumulated a nice balance in Jill's Love Bank.

As time went on the friendship deepened, and soon Jill realized that it had become more than a friendship for her. Finally, one day, she tentatively told Tom she was becoming attached to him.

"Jill," Tom replied, "I have been in love with you almost from the first time we met."

Within a few weeks Jill and Tom became deeply involved in an extramarital affair.

Jill had come full circle. Tom moved in to fill a need Harry had met beautifully before marriage. For some reason, Harry's attentiveness through conversation had fallen apart after the wedding. As Jill reflected on the whole thing, she thought, *What a shame I can't have these kinds of conversations with Harry. We had them once. Why not now?*

Why Won't My Husband Talk to Me?

I rarely have a man ask me, "Why isn't my wife talking to me?" but I often hear, "Why isn't my husband talking to me?" from women. Men do not seem to have as great a need for conversation with their wives as women do with their husbands. Women, on the other hand, seem to enjoy conversation for its own sake. Many women will spend hours with each other on the telephone, while men rarely call each other just to chat and be brought up-to-date. Meetings and luncheons and other gatherings where the entire purpose seems to be talking about their personal concerns bring women much pleasure. When men gather in conclaves, they tend to talk about practical matters, like fixing their cars, the best place to fish, or who holds first place in the sport of that season. They also like to exchange jokes and anecdotes. But they tend *not* to talk about themselves or their feelings.

Why, then, do men find it so easy to talk to women when they date them? One obvious reason is that they want to make a good impression, and of course the women want to do the same. During dating and courtship both eagerly demonstrate their abilities to be fun, witty, pleasant, and so on. Both feel highly motivated to discover what the other likes or dislikes. The man, especially, becomes uncharacteristically curious about his female companion. He wants to discover her feelings about things and to hear about her problems; he wants to know what will make her happy and content.

In this same vein he seeks to discover her interests. He wants to learn how to be attractive to her. Because he understands that she likes to be called, he promptly and regularly telephones whenever they cannot be together. This shows her how much he loves her and thinks of her.

As much as women enjoy conversation, they do not like men who spend the evening talking about only their own problems and achievements. I counsel a number of women who subscribe to one of the dating services in our area. After they use a dating service I frequently hear: "The guy was a *bore!* All he did was talk about himself."

This indicates that conversation that satisfies a woman's need must focus on the events of **her** day, people **she** may have encountered, and—

most of all—*how she feels about them.* She wants *verbal* attention, but she willingly gives the same attention to her husband and enjoys some conversation in which the man talks only about himself and what he has done.

Most important, a woman wants to be with someone who—in her perception—cares deeply about her and for her. When she perceives this kind of caring, she feels close to the person with whom she talks. In the female psyche, conversation blends with affection to help the woman feel united with the other person. She feels bonded to that person as long as the affection and conversations continue *on a daily basis.*

If a husband's job takes him out of town, the telephone can help maintain a sense of communication and closeness. But even if he calls home every night, when he returns, it's quite common for his wife to need a day or two to reestablish the bonding to her husband she had before he left. Women married to men who travel often tell me how hard they find adjusting to their spouses' return. One said, "It takes a day or two for me to feel close enough to make love."

Many—perhaps most—of the couples I counsel have problems that are job related. Jobs that require a lot of travel, like sales, airline positions, executive work, and the like, wreak havoc on marriages. The in-and-out pattern of the spouse on the move makes it difficult, if not impossible, for the other spouse to maintain a sense of oneness. Where *both* spouses often move about, it becomes twice the challenge to remain emotionally bonded.

It Takes Time to Communicate

If a husband seriously wants to meet his wife's need to feel close to him, he will give the task sufficient time and attention. I tell male clients they should learn to set aside fifteen hours a week to give their wives undivided attention. Many men look at me as if they think I'm losing my mind, or they just laugh and say, "In other words, I need a thirty-six-hour day." I don't bat an eye, but simply ask them how much time they spent giving their wives undivided attention during their courting days. Any bachelor who fails to devote something close to fifteen hours a week to his girlfriend faces the strong likelihood of losing her.

What happens on a typical date during courtship? A couple finds an activity that provides an excuse to get together. Usually they share a recreational activity—like playing racquetball or going to a movie or out to dinner. But the activity is incidental. They *really* want to get together to focus on each other. Most dates center around showing each other affection and having conversation.

When a courting couple shares their time, they usually have two basic, although possibly unconscious, goals. They try to (1) get to know each other more thoroughly, and (2) let each other know how much they care for each other.

Why should these goals be dropped *after* the wedding?

The couple desiring a happy marriage carries on with these functions and goals throughout their lifetimes. Primarily for the sake of the woman, they must set aside time to have dates with each other. Here's where my recommended fifteen hours comes in. A couple may include other activities in this period of time, but the primary activity should be conversation—private and intimate conversation without children or friends.

Without much time together, women especially lose the sense of intimacy they need and enjoy so much, and the Love Bank begins to be drained of funds. I settled on fifteen hours a week by asking female clients how much time they need with their husbands before they feel close and comfortable enough to enjoy sexual intimacy.

A given activity qualifies to be part of the fifteen-hour goal if you can affirmatively answer the question "Does this activity allow us to focus primarily on each other?" Going to see a movie for three hours does not meet that criterion. You may exchange some affection during the running of the film, but in most cases you cannot truly say that you focused attention on each other.

Activities like taking a walk, going to a restaurant, boating on a quiet pond, golfing, sunbathing at the beach—things of that nature—better qualify. Any recreational activity that requires intense concentration or so much exercise that conversation becomes difficult does not qualify.

If you engaged in conversation while riding together in the car, however, count it toward the fifteen hours. Do the same for shared meals that included no distraction from children or other sources.

During courtship women fall in love as a result of the time they spend exchanging conversation and affection. If a couple continues to engage in the activities that brought them together in the first place, their marriage will tend to be a good one. When two people get married, each partner has a right to expect the same loving care and attention that prevailed during courtship to continue after the wedding. Unfortunately, the common stereotype applied to many—perhaps most—marriages shows one or both spouses doing a complete flip-flop in actions or attitudes—before the "I do's" hardly died away. Of course, the stereotype lacks accuracy, because it usually takes several months or even years for things to change, but they do change. Why? Because in marriage, people do not make a commitment of time to each other. We know better, but we all tend to take our spouses for granted. The new pressures in life after marriage often catch us off guard, and we run out of time to care for the person to whom we have committed our love.

The "I can take my spouse for granted" syndrome explains why the "fantastic conversations" of the courtship can fade into a humdrum married existence that disappoints and disillusions. Every husband and wife need to sit down and meditate on this thought: *My partner married me because she or he thought the pleasing things I was doing during our courtship would continue for the rest of our lives. Am I holding up my end of this bargain?*

Most people who marry do not assume that their courtship has been a fantasy and that, after marriage, everything will become terrible. They marry because they have enjoyed what happened during the courtship so much that they want it to continue for life.

Granted, circumstances may change after the wedding. In the early days of our marriage, Joyce and I faced tight finances. I was still in school, yet I needed to support my wife and children. Joyce stayed home with the children, and every dollar counted. I had to ask myself, *What would Joyce like more: money to spend or time with me?* If I had put it to her in those terms, she may have opted for the money, because we had to pay our bills and keep the household going—another basic need in most women that we will examine closely in chapter 9. Fortunately we didn't let financial pressure come between us. In subsequent years, during my counseling experiences I would learn this truth: Money or a career should serve a marriage; a marriage should *never* serve money or a career. In many of the failed marriages I have observed, the couple abandoned their relationship to build a fortune. In the end they had a fortune at the expense of their marriage.

The great American scramble for more goodies as you move up the ladder of success becomes perhaps the deadliest enemy any family faces. What should be primary in a marriage: your relationship as man and woman, or your standard of living? We all know the "right" answer, but many couples still get it all backwards. They put their standard of living ahead of their relationship with the mistaken idea, "We will be happy if we can just get ahead." In many cases exactly the reverse happens. They reach a "higher standard of living" but at a terrible price.

Because Joyce and I decided to spend more time together, some other lifestyle changes had to take place. I'd seen the fallacy of judging things *only* from a financial standpoint, but I still had bills to pay. For us it meant cutting our standard of living.

The couple who spends extra hours on the job or moonlighting may be writing the death certificate for their marriage—or at least preparing to put it in the hospital. They need to realize that their relationship is the most important part of their quality of life.

Why Is Conversation So Important?

As we study the ten basic needs for men and women you'll begin to see that they all interrelate very closely. Because of this, if you fail to meet one of your spouse's needs, it may also influence your ability to fulfill another. For instance, imagine trying to successfully meet your partner's need for sex or affection without using verbal communication. Without conversation, the warm atmosphere and the deep physical relationship each partner needs could never be maintained!

Some people erroneously believe they can separate fulfillment of these basic marital needs. The wife whose husband won't talk may think it's fine if she just finds a friend to talk to her instead—farming out her needs but remaining faithful to her husband sexually may seem okay at first. The problem is that she inadvertently undermines her marriage by losing the bonding intimate conversation with her husband creates for her. Deep down she knows that if she is to feel united with him, he must talk to her.

"George, let's talk."

"What would you like to talk about?"

George's innocent inquiry would raise the ire of most women, if they heard it coming out of their husbands' mouths, because it shows how little a man seems to understand that conversation meets a woman's real need. He might understand Mary's aggravation better if she had a conversation like this with him:

"Mary, let's make love."

"Why, George? Are we ready to have children?"

When we see Mary's conversation with George about sex, we can begin to appreciate how ridiculous George's question about having a talk looks to a woman, yet in many average marriages, this same dialogue repeats frequently. Why? I believe it is because neither understands how the other looks at conversation.

Just as George finds sex enjoyable in its own right, Mary needs conversation. As with most women, it makes her feel more romantic love for George because she can deeply share her life with her husband. The atmosphere it creates contributes to her happiness. The man who takes time to talk to a woman will have an inside track to her heart.

George sees conversation primarily as a means to an end and not an end in itself. If he wants to find out how the bank account got overdrawn, you can be sure he'll talk to Mary, but he's not likely to talk about how nice the teller in the bank was to him, last time he went there. Women also understand that conversation has practical purposes, but they have a hard time explaining that they simply enjoy talking to someone.

While conversation does meet an emotional need for women, it also serves other purposes in building a relationship. It helps couples (1) communicate their needs to each other, and (2) learn how to meet each other's needs. When a husband and wife take part in conversation that really communicates this information about their needs, they learn to become more compatible. To start such a conversation, ask what your spouse thinks and feels. One evening you might use questions such as these: "What has made you feel good today? What has made you feel bad?" Then let your spouse know what made you feel good today and what made you feel bad.

69

When you share this kind of information, you will better understand what's going on in your spouse's world and his or her reactions to situations that influence you both. If something I do affects my wife negatively, I need to know it so I can eliminate that behavior and do something pleasing for her instead. Conversely, if I'm doing something right, I need to know that, too, so I can continue or even increase that action. Couples can't work too hard or too long at this process, because even doing something with the best intentions can backfire, if you don't keep in touch this way.

How to Keep from Growing Apart

I can personally testify to how a couple can change and grow apart if they don't maintain good conversation. When we married, I had just graduated from college, and Joyce had just finished her second year. After just two months of married life Joyce decided not to finish college and took a full-time job as a secretary. We had our first child when I completed two years of graduate school, and Joyce became a full-time homemaker. At the end of three more years of graduate school, I had a Ph.D., and we had two children.

Joyce began to develop her interest and ability in music while my career led me into psychology. She became a gospel recording artist and sought-after speaker and vocalist. I taught psychology, conducted research, and developed a counseling practice.

Soon I saw that we had little to talk about anymore. When I tried to tell her about my work, she tuned in for all of ten seconds and then was gone. I listened for about the same amount of time when she described her latest challenges. The Love Bank began to be debited. Her sphere of interests was becoming totally different from mine. In diagram form, the problem looked like Illustration 1.

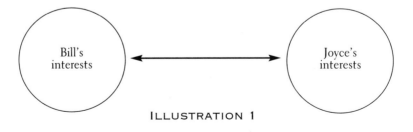

ILLUSTRATION 1

We recognized that we faced no minor problem and decided to do something about it before it got away from us. Our relationship was far more important to us than our career achievements. Instead we needed a situation you could diagram like Illustration 2.

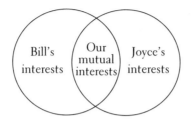

ILLUSTRATION 2

We both made an effort to become more involved in each other's sphere of interests. Since I was already interested in music and thoroughly enjoyed Joyce's concerts, I volunteered to help her prepare for her concerts and speaking engagements. Joyce became my interior decorator, using her talents in art. She decorated all my clinics and acted as hostess for seminars and clinic social events.

We learned to serve each other in our respective areas of interest. That didn't mean we tried to take over, tell each other what to do, or give each other a lot of unasked-for advice. With the new arrangement, we soon saw our spheres of interests beginning to overlap. Some of my sphere remained a mystery to her and vice versa, but now we had that overlapping area where we had *mutual* interests to share. We recovered the sense of oneness that we had while we were dating. Our Love Bank balance began to rise again.

In order to get more involved in each other's activities, we had to cut back in some areas of our own. This form of accommodation is essential in building compatibility.

To summarize the key points:

1. I have my sphere of interests, and my spouse has hers. If these do not overlap, we can only grow farther and farther apart.
2. Because there are only so many hours in the day and week, I have to choose: I can pursue interests that we share, or I can pursue

interests we do not share. If I do the latter, we will grow apart. If I do the former, we will grow together.

3. As I gain interests that are my spouse's interests we have much more to talk about. Conversation becomes easier and more interesting. I can meet her need for conversation with less and less effort. It becomes natural and spontaneous.

The above ideas sound almost simplistic, but amazingly many couples seem to remain unaware of them. They choose instead to follow the bad advice offered by some pop-psych writers or occasional talk-show guests working on their fourth or fifth marriages. Such would-be advisors urge husbands and wives to deliberately choose separate interests in an effort to "maintain space" and gain independence from each other. They try to sell the idea that if you interact and depend too much on each other you will lose your personal identity and personal sense of self-worth.

I believe this is one of the most damaging ideas being spread today. How can you have much to talk about if you only have separate interests? The argument for separate interests suggests that a couple has *more* to talk about as they share what they have been doing completely apart from each other. I wish it could be so; it would save me a lot of work in my counseling office. But my experience shows that a couple becomes far more likely to grow apart as their spheres of interests separate.

I'm not saying a husband and wife must spend every moment together and do everything together, but I do believe every marriage needs some mutual interests shared by both partners if they hope to communicate well. A marriage that sees husband and wife holding widely divergent interests may survive, but I have seen few that flourish under such circumstances.

All right, suppose you have committed yourselves to taking time for conversation, letting each other know what you like and don't like, using questions that probe for feelings and reactions, and seeking in every way you can to develop compatibility by developing mutual interests. These are all good goals, but you still face the challenge of making your conversations positive and beneficial. Some couples may battle a backlog of feelings and hang-ups because they have communicated so negatively or poorly in the past.

What goes into a good conversation? How do husbands and wives learn to converse in a way that is enjoyable for both of them? How can they learn to use their tongues to make deposits instead of withdrawals in each other's Love Bank?

Books abound on marital communication and the scope of this chapter can't cover all the topics and teachings available. Following, however, are several suggestions about basic things to avoid or include in your conversations. As I counsel couples I see these areas surfacing over and over.

The Enemies of Good Conversation

First, let's deal with the enemies of good conversation that make you *withdraw* love units from each other's Love Bank.

Enemy # 1: Using conversation to get your way at your spouse's expense

There's nothing wrong with asking for what you want from each other. But when your requests turn into demands, you've turned a corner that leads to Love-Bank withdrawals.

Whenever you make a demand, you are telling your spouse you don't really care how he or she feels when fulfilling it. You want what you want, and that's all that matters. Of course, you may have fifty reasons why it's just and proper for your spouse to give you what you want. But the bottom line is that you want your way, even if it is at your spouse's expense. I guarantee you, such conversation withdraws love units.

Demands do more than destroy your spouse's love for you, however. They also make it less likely that your spouse will do what you want at some later date. Even if you manage to make your spouse obey your command this time, you can bet that he or she will be on guard next time and attack fire with fire. A fight is almost sure to be the result of your demand, if not this time, next time. Demands are not only enemies of good conversation, they are also very foolish ways of getting what you may need, and even deserve, in your marriage.

Enemy #2: Using conversation to punish each other

Verbally punishing your spouse makes major Love-Bank withdrawals. It's nothing short of mental and emotional abuse. Frequently it causes more harm than physical abuse.

I have witnessed cases in which couples have developed key phrases especially designed to hurt each other. Once a partner utters such a phrase, name-calling begins, and both lose all control, blasting each other with every hurtful expression that comes to mind.

In most nonmarital relationships it is usually avoided. But in marriage, avoidance is impossible; over time, resentment from past verbal battles causes a married couple to hate each other.

If you feel angry and resentful, express your feelings by describing your expectations to your spouse. But remember, don't ever use verbal punishment. It only makes your spouse *less* willing to meet your needs in the future.

Enemy #3: Using conversation to force agreement to your way of thinking

Very few conversations are more irritating than those in which someone tries to force his opinion on you. This person seems unable to grasp the value of your right to make decisions. If you want your spouse to understand your feelings, you must express them somehow. But the accommodation of your feelings should not require your spouse's loss of personal values or judgment.

Never force your spouse to agree with you. If you cannot come to an agreement, learn to respect your husband's or wife's opinion and try to gain a greater understanding of its background. In the end, such respect will gain you a greater opportunity to share your position without risking withdrawals from the Love Bank.

Enemy #4: Dwelling on mistakes, past or present

In or outside marriage, most people resent denunciations, criticism, or corrections. If others tell us we have made a mistake, we often try to justify our failure or cast blame elsewhere.

On the other hand, if someone we care for explains that he or she would like us to meet a personal need, we are usually willing to help.

As long as we are not criticized, we can willingly accommodate others with some change in our behavior.

Mistakes are difficult to prove. What one person might call a mistake can seem correct from another's perspective. On the other hand, failure to meet the needs of another comes across more clearly. If my wife, Joyce, tells me that I am irritating, I should accept her statement at face value. After all, she is the best judge of her own feelings. When she makes such a comment, she has not necessarily criticized me, instead she has revealed the impact of my behavior on her feelings. My care for her is a gift, not a requirement. If I care for her feelings, I want her to help me learn how to behave in a way that meets her needs. But if she demands these changes in my behavior, she takes my generosity and care for granted, and it makes me feel defensive.

Harley's Third Law of Marriage sums it up this way:

> ## Caring partners converse in a caring way.

The Friends of Good Conversation

Now let's consider the friends of good conversation, which help you *deposit* love units into your Love Bank.

Friend # 1: Developing interest in each other's favorite topics of conversation

In my experience counseling couples, I have found that even the most introverted people become talkative when we discuss certain subjects. Women may notice that their quiet husbands come out of their shells when out with a few good male friends.

I once counseled a couple who were about to experience divorce, because the wife could no longer accept her husband's silence. In my office, alone with me, the man turned into a chatterbox. However, when his wife joined us, he became stone quiet. Certain subjects of interest to him brought him out. Once these subjects were introduced, he could then continue to converse on a wide range of other subjects.

Many people need to begin their conversation with subjects that "prime the pump." Once under way, they can switch to less stimulating subjects and enjoy keeping their end of the conversation.

Friend #2: Balancing the conversation

In the case I just mentioned, I had both husband and wife estimate the amount of time they spoke, and in a ten-minute conversation, she was to allow him about five minutes. At first she expected him to say nothing during his time. But once they included subjects that interested him, he filled his half of the ten minutes. Until she was required to balance their conversation, giving him an equal amount of time to speak, she remained unaware of her habit of interrupting him.

Those who monopolize conversation create an unwanted habit in their spouses—silence. Therefore, if you want a good conversation, be sensitive to each other's right to "have the floor." It may take your spouse two or three seconds to begin a sentence, but allow whatever time is necessary. Also, remember to wait until your spouse completes a thought before commenting on it.

Friend #3: Using conversation to inform, investigate, and understand your spouse

One of the most valuable uses of marital conversation is to create emotional closeness. The topics of conversation you choose have a great bearing on the intimacy of your relationship.

If you have a superficial relationship, you are probably avoiding conversation that will help you learn to adjust to each other. You may deliberately give each other *misinformation*. You may *discourage investigation*. You may be *afraid to be understood* by your spouse. These common weaknesses lead to a serious and often disastrous failure to adjust to each other's needs. If you want a satisfying marriage, you must use some of your conversational time to *inform, investigate,* and *understand* each other.

Inform each other of your personal interests and activities, desiring to bring each other into your spheres of interest. Keep calendars of your activities for the day and plans for your future, and share them with each other. Don't keep your life secret from your spouse.

Investigate each other's personal feelings and attitudes without necessarily trying to change each other. You can learn much from each other without expecting any changes at all! If you criticize or ridicule your spouse's feelings or attitudes, they will be more difficult to express in the future. Instead encourage each other to be open and vulnerable by being respectful and sensitive.

Understand each other's motivation in life—what makes you happy and sad. Learn about each other's "hot" and "cold" buttons, so you can bring the best out in each other and avoid the worst. One of the most important ways for you to care for your spouse is to change your behavior to promote pleasure and avoid pain for your spouse.

Friend #4: Giving each other undivided attention

One of the quickest ways for a husband to infuriate his wife is to carry on a conversation while watching football. She becomes angry because he does not pay close attention to her. Instead, he's more interested in the football game.

The conversation a woman needs from her husband requires his *undivided attention.* As I discussed earlier in this chapter, I usually recommend that each week every married couple set aside fifteen hours for the purpose of giving each other their undivided attention. Don't watch football during that time!

Conversation Tips for Husbands and Wives

As a caring husband, a man converses with his wife in a way that enables her to reveal her deepest feelings. Through conversation he learns to meet many of her needs. But the *conversation itself* meets one of her most important marital needs: She simply wants him to talk to her.

I will end this chapter with a list that summarizes the ways you can care for your spouse with conversation. We've dealt with all of them: Now it's time to put them into action.

1. Remember how it was when you were dating. You both still need to exhibit that same intense interest in each other and in what you have to say—especially about your feelings.

2. A woman has a profound need to engage in conversation about her concerns and interests with someone who—in her perception—cares deeply about her and for her.

3. Men, if your job keeps you away from home overnight or for days on end, think about changing jobs. If you cannot, find ways to restore the intimacy of your marriage each time you return from an absence, so that your wife can begin to feel comfortable with you again. (If your wife does most of the traveling, the same principle applies.)

4. Get into the habit of spending fifteen hours each week alone with your spouse giving each other undivided attention. Spend much of that time in natural, but essential, conversation.

5. Remember, most women *fall in love* with men who have set aside time to exchange conversation and affection with them. They *stay in love* with men who continue to meet those needs.

6. Financial considerations should not interfere with time for conversation. If you don't have the time to be alone to talk, your priorities are not arranged correctly.

7. Never use conversation as a form of punishment (ridicule, name calling, swearing, or sarcasm). Conversation should be constructive, not destructive.

8. Never use conversation to force your spouse to agree with your way of thinking. Respect your spouse's feelings and opinions, especially when yours are different.

9. Never use conversation to remind each other of past mistakes. Avoid dwelling on present mistakes as well.

10. Develop interest in each other's favorite topics of conversation.

11. Learn to balance your conversation. Avoid interrupting each other and try to give each other the same amount of time to talk.

12. Use your conversation to *inform, investigate,* and *understand* each other.

When you meet your wife's need for conversation, you come to understand each other more clearly and learn what it takes to meet each other's needs. That in turn enables you to deposit love units in each other's Love Banks, which creates and sustains romantic love. The conversational skill is a must if you want to be irresistible to each other.

Questions for Him

1. Do I spend time talking to my wife? Is our time spent together near the fifteen-hour goal? Should we make changes?
2. Do I share interests with my wife? How can I improve?
3. Does my career take me away from my wife? How can I change?

Questions for Her

1. Do I miss anything from our dating days? Do we still have the kind of communication we shared then?
2. Am I doing anything that hinders conversation? Do I have a job that requires much travel? Do I talk too much? What can I do to improve such a situation?
3. What interests do I share with my husband? What do we talk about together? Are there any other areas we need to share?

To Consider Together

1. Are our spheres of interests totally separate, or do they overlap? If they overlap, what areas of mutual interest do we have? Do we communicate about them enough?
2. How can we rearrange our schedules to work toward a goal of fifteen hours a week of real communication together?
3. What communication tips in this chapter should we use to improve communication in our marriage?

6

RECREATIONAL COMPANIONSHIP

"Hi, Cindy, this is Alan."

"Hello! How nice of you to call." Her voice sounded warm and cheerful.

"I have tickets for the Bruins-Bears game at the Rose Bowl on Saturday. Would you like to go with me?"

"That sounds great! What time?"

They made the date, and Alan smiled after he hung up. He and Cindy had dated twice in the four weeks they had known each other. This would be the first "sports date," and he felt pleased that she sounded so eager to go. He didn't know many girls who liked football.

They had a great time at the game. Cindy seemed to understand enough about the game to know what was happening, and they even discussed some of the plays afterward at the coffee shop.

That autumn they took in several more games in addition to a half-dozen movies. Cindy's taste in films pleased Alan, too, and the romance was progressing nicely. By mid-winter Alan felt convinced he had found the right girl—at last. The weekend his car broke down doubly confirmed it in his mind. He called Cindy to explain.

"Honey, I'm sorry. My car won't run, and I've got to try to fix it this afternoon to have it for work on Monday."

"Oh, that's okay. Why don't I get my roommate to run me over, and I'll give you a hand. I'll bring coffee and sandwiches."

The car repair turned into one of their best dates ever. Cindy handed Alan tools and generally made herself useful while they talked and joked.

This girl, thought Alan, *is really special.*

They arranged their wedding for the first week in May. On their honeymoon they went to the mountains to do a little hiking together. The summer passed blissfully with some trips to the beach, and everything went very well—until football season. At the last minute, Cindy begged off on going with Alan to see UCLA play Arizona State. By the end of the season, the only other games she attended with him were Oregon State and the big one against University of Southern California.

So one night at dinner, early in December, Alan brought this turn of events to Cindy's attention. "I thought you liked football," he complained.

"Oh, honey, I do. I guess I just don't enjoy it quite as much as you do. A couple of games during the season is enough for me," she replied.

"Oh," said Alan flatly, not sure how to handle this new and unexpected information.

"I've been meaning to ask you about something," she continued. "The county art museum has a special exhibit of Spanish Renaissance painters this month. Would you go with me?"

"Yeah, sure, I guess so," Alan replied.

Over the next year, Alan discovered that the things he liked to do and the things Cindy *really* liked to do had little in common. Her interest in auto repairs had evaporated practically overnight, and he felt lucky to get her to even one football game. Meanwhile, she insisted that he take her to more art museums and an occasional concert or opera. Alan balked at all this culture, and gradually they arrived at the point where they rarely did much together except go out to dinner once in a while.

At the end of two years of marriage, they had an agreement that he would spend an evening or an afternoon each week with his friends, and she would do the same with her friends. Alan would have preferred to spend more "fun" time with Cindy, but she seemed quite content with the arrangement.

Hurt and bewildered, Alan often asked himself, *I wonder what made her change?*

How Important Is Recreational Compatibility?

In counseling sessions I have often heard variations of the saga of Cindy and Alan. Cindy, of course, never really "changed." It is not uncommon for women, when they are single, to join men in pursuing their interests. They find themselves hunting, fishing, playing football, and watching movies they would never have chosen on their own. After marriage wives often try to interest their husbands in activities more to their own liking. If their attempts fail, they may encourage their husbands to continue their recreational activities without them. I consider that option very dangerous to a marriage, because men place surprising importance on having their wives as recreational companions. The TV stereotypes paint the opposite picture, showing husbands out with the boys on fishing trips saying, "It doesn't get any better than this." My counseling files say it can get a lot better. In fact, among the five basic male needs, **spending recreational time with his wife is second only to sex for the typical husband.**

People often challenge my claim, saying they know any number of happily married couples whose recreational interests are totally different. But these people do not necessarily know the couples in their most honest moments. I have counseled married couples who maintain an excellent image right up to the moment of divorce. They successfully hide their deepest needs from themselves and others until it is too late.

Sometimes recreational tastes overshadow deep personal needs. By nature men and women often seem to have divergent tastes when it comes to having fun. Men seem to enjoy recreations that involve more risk, more adventure, and more violence than the recreational interests of women. Men typically enjoy football, boxing, hunting, fishing, hang gliding, scuba diving, snowmobiling, and skydiving. They tend to prefer movies with sex and violence or jokes about sex and violence. Men usually do not mind sweat, dirt, body odor, or belching. Most women find all of this unpleasant and tasteless.

After informally polling hundreds of female clients over the years, I have concluded that the all-time favorite recreation for most women is going out to dinner. They also like picnics, walks, romantic movies, cultural events, and shopping.

In the realm of athletics women tend to participate in individual rather than team sports. Golf, tennis, track, aerobic dancing, swimming, and racquetball come high on the lists of many active women. With spectator sports, things are changing. More and more women now enjoy football, basketball, and baseball, to name a few of the major sports.

The classic struggle finds the woman trying to "clean up the man's act," making him shave, dress more neatly, talk more gently, and so on. When she moves in on his recreational life, he may conclude she wants to spoil things or at least cut down on his fun. He still loves her, but she begins to cramp his style. To avoid that, he spends some time with men only. This allows him to retain his sense of identity as a man, but it also means that some of his most enjoyable activities are done without his wife present.

In addition, family responsibilities cause tension. Because he only has so much time, a husband must choose between his buddies and his family. For example, when his vacation comes up, will he spend it going on a hunting trip with some of the guys, or will he stay home with his family and visit amusement parks?

When a man tries to split his time between these two choices, he often finds that his family (especially his wife) resents the time he spends with his male friends. A three-day hunting trip once a year in the fall is still something a wife commonly wishes her husband would not do.

If he's going to take the time off, she thinks, *he should spend it with me and the children.*

What Happened to Cindy and Alan?

Men often get married expecting their wives to meet their strong need for recreational companionship. Frequently they are disappointed, as Alan discovered in our opening story.

Where could the scenario have gone from where we left Alan and Cindy—both going in separate directions, with Alan feeling disappointed and wondering why Cindy had "changed"? In some marriages, a man like Alan would just trudge off alone to watch his Bruin gridders and make the best of it. But all too commonly Alan winds up in a bowling league, perhaps, with some of his buddies, where he meets Barbara, who just loves sports of all kinds. They have a cup of coffee as they compare bowling scores, and before you know it, they are good friends. (After all, bowling leagues last for months.)

If Alan doesn't watch it, he will find himself in an affair with Barbara, who promises to meet all those recreational needs Alan expects Cindy to meet. If the scenario plays out to its ironic end, Alan will divorce Cindy to marry Barbara and—you guessed it—*she* will suddenly decide concerts, or maybe croquet matches, are more fun than bowling or football. I have seen this exact irony come back to haunt men who thought an affair, divorce, and remarriage would solve their problems.

Again I must emphasize that men like Alan don't wander into an affair out of anger or revenge. Alan felt hurt by Cindy's change of behavior, but he didn't begrudge her the right to revert to her real interests. The danger in all of this lies in the two of them simply continuing to grow farther and farther apart. That common pattern at its worst can lead to an affair and divorce; the wise couple will avoid it in their marriage or correct it as soon as they find it.

Once in a while, however, I meet a man like Hank, who genuinely resented his wife for the loss of her recreational companionship after they got married. Hank was a health-and-fitness buff. One day out on the jogging track he met Joanne, and they went a couple of miles together, just to be sociable. Joanne's ability to hold an eight-minute-mile pace impressed Hank. A week or so later he felt doubly impressed when he met her on the tennis court and noted that she had a better backhand than his. Soon they started jogging together all the time and became a familiar mixed-doubles team at the tennis club. Not surprisingly, they fell in love and got married. After the marriage, Joanne started begging off on going out for a daily jog with Hank. She also found it inconvenient to make their tennis matches every Saturday. In just a few months Joanne seemed to lose total interest in physical fitness. She preferred just staying home and watching television.

Hank couldn't believe it. Not surprisingly, he refused to take it lying down. He became so angry about her refusal to jog with him that eventually they came to me for marital counseling.

After listening to their story, I asked Joanne, "It looks as though one of his basic understandings upon entering into the marriage contract with you was that you would jog with him. Would it be *that* hard for you to go jogging now and then?"

"I jogged with him before," Joanne explained, "in order to be near him. But I never thought that jogging made him fall in love with me. We just happened to be jogging, and I believed he came to love me for who I was. When we got married, I didn't think jogging had to be part of the deal. I don't need or want jogging any longer."

I felt a little puzzled at first by her unwillingness to negotiate even slightly to save their marriage. Later, however, she added some explanations that helped me make more sense of it. In their arguments over her refusal to jog, Hank had gotten so angry that Joanne had seen an ugly side of him she didn't like at all. She had no idea he could act that way. As Hank ranted and raved his balance in Joanne's Love Bank suffered hefty withdrawals. While Joanne cast Hank as the heavy, he had his side of the story, too. Joanne's stubborn refusal to do any more jogging or tennis playing caused her balance in his Love Bank to drop sharply as well. It seems incredible, but they refused all help. For want of some jogging together, their marriage ended in a march to the divorce court.

Where do stories like this leave us? Every couple has the choice to let unmet needs hamper or even ruin their relationship, or they can decide to preserve their marriage. Divorce seldom, if ever, provides a good answer to any marital problem. Limping along in disappointment and bittersweet frustration doesn't do any better. A mature coming together to meet each other's needs is always the best solution. Let's take a look at how this can be done regarding the man's need for recreational companionship.

The Spheres of Interest Revisited

Do you remember the spheres of interests I described in the last chapter? There I showed you the importance of mutual interests and the role they play in communication. When Joyce and I drifted apart in ours, I showed you how we changed some interests and activities so that our spheres became closer and finally overlapped. Once this happened, we had *mutual* interests and better communication.

The rules that work for conversation also work for recreation, and Joyce and I faced challenges in this area, too. For example, when I was younger I loved to play chess. I started at age four and eventually became president of my university club, where I was first board.

After I married I gave up chess tournaments because Joyce didn't play and had no interest in learning. Chess is an extremely time-consuming game, and much as I loved it, I decided we could better spend our recreational time doing something we both enjoyed. I thought we would both enjoy tennis, since we had spent countless hours playing during courtship days. During the first year of marriage, however, Joyce announced, "Bill, I don't really enjoy tennis that much anymore. I think I would prefer other ways of spending time together."

Joyce's turnaround on tennis came as a complete surprise to me. We had dated for six years before we married, and I thought I knew her very well. We had enjoyed lots of tennis, as well as other sports. I hadn't realized I enjoyed them much more than Joyce had. Because she wanted to be with me, she accommodated me by doing what I wanted to do. The trouble was, she almost always lost. No matter what we did competitively—tennis, bowling, checkers, or whatever—she rarely won. So early in our marriage, she did the right thing. She let me know this wasn't fun anymore. From that point on our recreational activities became much more noncompetitive. We switched to group sporting events, like volleyball, where we could play on the same team, and expanded our interests in films, plays, concerts, dining out, sightseeing, and enjoying nature.

Because we stayed together in pursuit of recreation, today we spend almost all our recreational time with each other. The outcome could have been quite different if I had stuck to tennis and chess and let Joyce go her way. We would have grown apart, each experiencing our most enjoyable moments of fun and relaxation without the other. When I counsel married couples, I can't emphasize too strongly what a mistake this can be. Instead of making steady deposits in each other's Love Banks by having fun together, the couple with separate recreational interests misses a golden opportunity. They often spend some of their most enjoyable moments in the company of *someone else*, with the distinct possibility of building a Love Bank account with that person. Since everyone has an account in your Love Bank, it stands to reason that the person with whom you share your most enjoyable moments will build the largest account. If you want a fulfilling marriage, that person **must** be your spouse.

How to Find Mutual Recreational Interests

In counseling situations, when I explain the importance of mutual recreational interests, some couples have no problem discovering things to do together. Others, however, appear at a total loss. They are just too different and, "Besides *he* simply won't give up his bowling team" and, "*She* absolutely must continue her bridge club on Tuesday afternoons."

I smile and say, "No problem. Imagine that around each of you is drawn an invisible circle encompassing all your recreational interests and sources of enjoyment. Within each of your circles there are bound to be some interests that overlap. You may not enjoy these equally, but to some degree they please both of you. Once you find these sources of pleasure, you have your overlapping area of interests to pursue together."

Next, I ask couples to complete my Recreational Enjoyment Inventory (a copy can be found in appendix C). It's a list of 125 recreational activities with space to indicate how much a husband or wife likes or dislikes each one. Couples can add activities to the list that are not included and rate them as well.

When the inventory is completed, the activities that have been rated enjoyable by *both* husband and wife are identified. This exercise usually produces a list of ten or fifteen activities the wife and the husband can enjoy together. In the weeks to come I ask them to schedule these activities into their recreational time. Some of these choices will be things he may like a bit more than she does, and vice versa, but in every case, they will both be depositing love units as they spend recreational time together.

No one can do everything he or she would like in life. There's just not enough time. Every person's recreational time amounts to making choices that will leave out other opportunities. Why not select those activities you can share?

Can a Wife Be Her Husband's Best Friend?

When a couple draws up their master list of mutually enjoyable activities, there are many surprises. Some are activities that neither have ever experienced before. They simply sounded like they might be enjoyable. Other surprises are activities that the couple didn't realize were mutually enjoyable. They both thought the other disliked doing them.

But another type of surprise is finding that something they are already doing together is unpleasant for one of them. What are they to do with that activity? My Policy of Mutual Appeal covers that situation:

> ## Engage in only those recreational activities that both you and your spouse can enjoy together.

It's a tough rule, but one that I insist must be followed by couples who come to me for counseling. Not only does it rule out some activities that you may be doing together, but it also rules out all recreational activities that you are doing apart that only one of you enjoys.

You can probably imagine the abuse I've taken to even suggest such a thing! It means, for example, that a husband might have to give up "Monday Night Football." Men who thought I was trying to help them out by encouraging their wives to join them in their favorite activities are faced with the prospect of abandoning those activities entirely. I've lost the respect of many potential converts on this one. Many have felt that I've gone too far.

But once you think it through, you have to agree with me, at least on principle. If you were to find recreational activities that both you and your spouse could enjoy together, just as much as you enjoy your favorite activities now, it would definitely improve your feelings for each other. And that's the goal I'm after. What's more important, the quality of your marriage or "Monday Night Football"? In some cases that's the choice you have.

You can't do everything. Out of thousands of possible activities, there will probably exist only a few hundred that my wife and I would enjoy thoroughly. I cannot possibly do all those hundreds of things that my wife and I *would* enjoy. Why, then, should I waste my time doing the things my wife finds no pleasure in? This policy of engaging in only mutually appealing activities is not a summons to a lifetime of misery and deprivation. It simply means choosing activities I already enjoy by taking my wife's feelings into account. Why should I wish to gain at her expense, when we can gain together?

Although some marriage counselors might not agree with me, I believe that a husband and wife should be each other's best friend. Some would say that you cannot force this kind of issue, but the principle I've introduced in this chapter does indeed "force" a husband and wife to be "best friends," through the sheer time they spend with each other. My policy of "mutual interests only" says a husband and wife cannot engage in most recreational activities unless they share them. The only exception to this rule allows the husband or wife to engage in some activity that helps achieve an important goal that's agreed to with mutual enthusiasm.

A key example here would be time spent with children. In our own family, Joyce has greatly supported the time I spend with our son in recreational activities. Steve and I have learned scuba diving together. We have also gone snowmobiling, soaring, hunting, and skiing. Joyce has never expressed or felt any resentment when I have been out together with Steve in these recreational pastimes. Even though Joyce and I were not physically together in these activities, we achieved an important mutual goal: good parenting. Because of that, she could feel genuinely happy about my activities.

The same was true when Joyce helped our daughter, Jennifer, develop her interest and ability in horsemanship. They spent hundreds of hours together attending horse shows throughout the state. Once again I completely supported her efforts, since through them she, too, achieved the goal of good parenting.

When you follow the "mutually appealing activities" rule, you insure the continuation of deposits in your spouse's Love Bank. Some of my best feelings occur when I pursue a favorite recreational goal. If I share it with my wife, I will associate those good feelings with her, and as my love grows for her our marriage becomes strengthened. If I share these emotions with someone else, I will also associate those feelings with that other person. By doing this, I have lost an opportunity to develop love for my spouse and risk developing love for another woman.

Many spouses—particularly husbands—find my Policy of Mutual Appeal hard to put into practice. Just the thought of giving up their very favorite activities like hunting or football causes depression to set in for many men. I can understand, because men need recreation in their lives to keep going. They work hard all day and look forward to the relatively few hours of enjoyment they can schedule themselves. Then some marriage counselor comes along and tells them they cannot do the very things they believe help keep them going.

Still I encourage such men to try my plan for a few months, reminding them that I have not told them to give up recreational pleasures. I simply advise them to include their wives and choose activities they both enjoy. It's not a matter of giving up all the pleasures of life. Instead, a man must simply replace his old pastimes with some he can share with his spouse or make her a part of the ones he already enjoys.

In making the changes, a wife needs to be alert to the possibility that breaking a recreational habit can put some men into a state of withdrawal. He may miss it terribly at first, but once he fights his way through, he comes to enjoy mutually appealing activities even more. This is because one of his basic emotional needs is being met when his wife is his recreational companion.

On the wife's side, too, some conflict may occur in making these changes. When she asks her husband to give up his bowling night to stay with her, at first she may wonder if she's made a great mistake. She didn't mean to force herself on him, although she wants his companionship. Halfway through the first night, she may want to tell him to return to the league, because she feels guilty for taking him away from something she knows he truly enjoys and deserves.

She needs to hang in there as they develop new interests together, and her husband needs to be patient with her as she tries to learn one of his favorite activities. If, for one or both of you, an activity fails after the first time or two, don't give up. Take the time required to gain some skill. Suppose a wife begins to take up skiing to please her husband. She needs time to build up the muscles required and learn the techniques that make her proficient. If he pushes her on too fast, she may come to resent it and will quickly turn away from the sport. With time she might have found it very enjoyable.

However, if she tries skiing, gains some proficiency, then still dislikes it, the wife should have the freedom to tell her husband, "I've tried it. I still don't like it. Let's try something else."

Give yourselves time to adjust and to try new pastimes. You may have some difficulty accommodating these changes, but you'll find your marriage well worth the effort. In my counseling experiences I've found that couples who limit their recreational activities to those they do together make tremendous gains in compatibility. They also deposit scores of love units.

How Much Time Should You Spend in Recreation?

One of the secrets to efficiency is learning to do several things at once. In marriage, however, such an effort can become a great cause of resentment. For example, the fifteen hours you and your spouse schedule to give each other undivided attention should not be peppered with calls to the office or errands that distract your attention from each other.

On the other hand, recreational activities can become a part of this time without causing any resentment if the activity is not too distracting. When couples are courting, they tend to combine conversation and affection with recreational activities. It's a very natural blend that increases the pleasure that couples experience when they're together.

I encourage couples to try to use at least part of their fifteen hours for recreational activities. The only condition that must be met is that the activity cannot prevent a couple from giving each other undivided attention. If a favorite activity is too distracting to qualify, then a couple must schedule time outside their fifteen hours to engage in it together.

The policy that urges us to make our spouses primary recreational companions is not unbearably painful or unrealistic. In fact, it's the policy we followed when we first fell in love with them. Instead, the Policy of Mutual Appeal invites both spouses to a new level of intimacy and enjoyment of each other. Harley's Fourth Law of Marriage puts it this way:

> The couple that plays together
> stays together.

Questions for Her

1. Do you believe your husband puts as much emphasis on having you for a recreational companion as this chapter claims? If you answer no, has he possibly sent you signals that you have not received?

2. Which of the following describes your marriage?
   a) He goes his way, I go mine.
   b) We seem to do as much together as most couples do.
   c) We are close to or at the fifteen-hour level.
3. Can you think of any recreational pastime you would be willing to give up in order to spend more time with your husband? Could he do the same?

Questions for Him

1. Which of the following describes your marriage?
   a) She goes her way, I go mine.
   b) Without my nights out with the guys, I don't think I could make it.
   c) We aren't close to spending fifteen hours a week together, but I would like to try.
   d) We're close to the fifteen-hour mark.
2. Does limiting your recreational time strictly to your wife sound threatening to you? If so, try to put your feelings down on paper to see exactly what bothers you.
3. What are you willing to give up to spend more recreational time with your wife? What do you think she would give up?

To Consider Together

1. The most important assignment has been described in this chapter. Use the form, Recreational Enjoyment Inventory, found in appendix C to help you discover mutually appealing activities.
2. After identifying activities you both enjoy, schedule time to try each of them. Narrow them down to five or ten that you enjoy the most.

7

HONESTY AND OPENNESS

Dorothy felt both perplexed and enchanted by Frank's mystique: She had never met a more private man, and he often evaded her questions. Near the end of a date she might ask him where he was going or what he was planning to do. He would just wink, smile knowingly, and say, "I'll call you tomorrow."

Frank's behavior seemed a bit odd, but Dorothy told herself that everybody has a right to privacy. Certainly Frank had a right to keep *some* things to himself.

Truth be told, Frank had several things he kept to himself—specifically other girlfriends he did not want Dorothy to know about. When he couldn't conveniently evade her questions, he took pains to mislead her by telling her about nonexistent projects he had to complete at work. His true projects were dates with other women. Sometimes Dorothy suspected him of seeing someone else, but he made such a big thing out of his right to privacy that she felt guilty whenever she questioned his honesty.

Besides, Frank had a lot of the other things Dorothy wanted in a man. He was affectionate and charming. Other women cast envious looks when she walked into a party with such a tall, good-looking fellow. To ice the cake, he had an excellent income and spent money on her generously. When Frank proposed, all these pluses far outweighed his "I need my privacy" minus.

He'll tell me everything after we're married, Dorothy thought.

As it turned out, Frank's behavior did not change after the wedding. In fact, it seemed to become a bigger problem, because now that they lived together Frank had more occasions than ever to be secretive.

Interestingly enough, all this need for privacy did not mean Frank saw another woman. Once he made the marriage commitment, he dropped his other girlfriends to "settle down." But he still reserved the "right" to get home from work when he felt like it. Since his job involved an irregular schedule, Dorothy could seldom plan much of anything. Frank would call, but would only say, "I'll be late—maybe by six-thirty. I'm not sure." Dorothy quickly learned she was part of the "keep dinner warm in the oven" brigade. Once he did get home, Frank seemed to lose the charm that dazzled her during courtship. He had little to say when it came down to making plans.

"Can I invite the Morgans for dinner Saturday night?" Dorothy would ask.

"Not sure," Frank would reply. "I'll have to see—it's a busy week."

And so it went—from frustration to depression for Dorothy. Frank remained faithful enough, and he really had nothing to hide. For some reason, however—known only to him—he didn't want to share what he was doing or thinking.

"At the wedding our pastor said in marriage two become one," Dorothy told her friend Marge. "But Frank and I really can't be one if he won't share with me. I've asked him to go talk with our pastor with me, but he won't hear of it, and he forbids me to go alone. He tells me people at church will find out and misunderstand."

Mistrust Destroys Her Sense of Security

Dorothy and Frank are headed for trouble unless he realizes he has to change. If Frank insists on going on with his routine, he will only manage to slowly empty most of his Love Bank account with his wife. When his Love Bank account gets dangerously low, Dorothy will become a vulnerable target for a man who knows how to make her feel trusting and secure.

A sense of security is the bright golden thread woven through all of a woman's five basic needs. If a husband does not keep up honest and open communication with his wife, he undermines her trust and eventually destroys her security.

To feel secure, a wife must trust her husband to give her accurate information about his past, the present, and the future. What has he done? What is he thinking or doing right now? What plans does he have? If she can't trust the signals he sends (or if, as in the case of Frank, he refuses to send any signals), she has no foundation on which to build a solid relationship. Instead of adjusting to him, she always feels off balance; instead of growing up *with* him, she grows *away* from him.

The wife who can't trust her husband to give her the information she needs also lacks a means of negotiating with him. Negotiation between a husband and wife forms an essential building block to the success of any marriage, but without honesty and openness a couple can resolve or decide very little.

Suppose, for example, a wife wants to plan the family's next vacation. She asks her husband, "Where would you like to go, camping or to the resort?"

Her husband thinks to himself, *I know she'd rather go to the resort, but I hate it there.* However, he says to her, "Let's go to the resort."

So they go to the resort, and her husband sits around grumpy for two weeks, muttering about how they could have bought better camping equipment for the same amount they are spending on "being fancy."

The above scenario seems the stuff of which sitcoms are made, and these stories strike a chord with viewers because they seem so real. In a marriage that lacks honesty and openness, however, the lines of the "actors" sound less amusing.

Does Your Spouse Know You Better Than Anyone?

I tell couples I counsel that honesty is one of the most important qualities in a successful marriage. When you are married, you must send each other accurate messages and receive accurate responses.

One or both spouses often make the major mistake of feeling one way and responding in another. When you fail to respond the way you actually feel, your mate's adjustment to you will not hit the target. Husbands and wives often use the expression "Where are you coming from?" to find out how the other feels. If you project that you are "coming from" a particular place, your spouse will aim there with an appropriate accommodation. If in fact you really come from "somewhere else," your mate winds up missing the target, and you both end up frustrated.

A simple example shows Helen asking Harry, "How are you feeling— better?"

Harry grunts and says, "Yeah . . . yeah, yeah, I'm fine."

"Then let's go to a movie!"

"Can't you give me any peace? I work hard all day, get indigestion, and now you want me to run out to a movie!"

Whenever and wherever your mate asks you how you feel, tell the truth. It is foolish to lie out of fear that you will hurt your spouse's feelings (or possibly hurt your own pride). Your mate has a right to your innermost thoughts. Your mate should know you better than anyone else in the world—even your parents.

"Knowing you" includes your good and bad feelings, your frustrations, your problems and fears—anything that is on your mind. The Bible calls it "two becoming one"; we psychologists label it "achieving good marital compatibility."

When a wife hears lies from her husband, it knocks her response mechanism out of kilter. Suppose, for example, Barry lies to Barbara and says he loves the way she has her hair styled. So about a month later Barbara spends sixty-five dollars getting it cut, touched up, and set. She comes home and says, "I got my hair done, like it?"

"Uh, oh, yeah, honey, it's fine, just fine."

Barbara senses that he isn't thrilled and can't figure it out. Really, deep down, Harry doesn't like her hairstyle at all. He just told her that to make her happy. Now she doesn't feel happy at all, because she detects the underlying negative tone in his voice. His words say one thing, but he feels another. Barbara is confused by the contradiction.

Three Kinds of Lying Husbands

After years of counseling, I have discovered three basic types of dishonest behavior in husbands:

1. The "born" liar

From an early age, he has continually told small lies about inconsequential matters. Such a liar reports that he was reading when, in fact he was sleeping. He fabricates stories about events in his past and constantly distorts the truth in subtle ways that seem almost unnoticeable—at first. One can usually catch the born liar easily enough by doing a little simple checking. But be warned. When confronted, he usually excuses himself by pleading "a poor memory." A chronic liar finds it nearly impossible to consistently admit the truth about himself.

Such dishonesty will severely disrupt a marriage. Because his behavior is so ingrained, it probably will not change. Some of these men begin to improve during middle age and feel a certain guilt for their past dishonesty, but others remain dishonest the rest of their lives.

2. The "avoid trouble" liar

He doesn't lie all the time, only when there is pressure or a significant problem.

Suppose a husband has gone through the week neglecting his responsibility to secure a baby-sitter for Saturday night's outing. On Saturday morning, his wife asks him, "Oh, honey, did you remember to call Gail about baby-sitting tonight?"

"It's all taken care of, dear," he replies. To himself he thinks, *No need to get chewed out about my irresponsibility. I can call Gail in a little while and set it up.* But the morning goes by devoted to chores, and that afternoon a favorite team is on the tube, and thoughts of calling a sitter get pushed far into the back of his mind. Evening comes, but no baby-sitter.

"What happened?" his wife demands.

"It was all set up," he lies. "She must have forgotten."

His wife calls Gail, who denies that she ever got a call. The wife hangs up the phone and asks for an explanation.

"I can't understand it," our liar pleads. "Why would she lie about it? I don't think we ought to use her anymore."

The "avoid trouble" liar as well as the "born liar" have one thing in common. Their lying is rarely thought out, but rather impulsive and poorly planned. These people usually have what psychologists call a character disorder. They habitually distort reality with no apparent remorse unless they are caught. Then they often fabricate the remorse to get people to "forgive and forget."

Unlike the "born liar," the liar who wants to avoid trouble only periodically lies in his marriage when he feels he is under pressure. Sometimes it is possible to bring this type of liar into honest communication by making his wife aware of the way stress triggers a dishonest reaction. She is able to experience a more honest communication as the stresses in his life are reduced.

3. The "protector" liar

This man believes the truth would be just too much for his wife. So he lies in order to "protect" her.

For example, the family faces a financial emergency, but only the husband knows of it because he handles the checkbook. The "protector liar" husband might decide to borrow money without telling his wife. *Why should she lose any sleep over something like this?* he reasons. *The problem is only temporary—I know I can handle it.*

So he continues to lie to his wife, saying things are fine, when in fact he puts himself under tremendous stress. With strenuous effort he manages to pay back the loan, and his wife never knows—but at what price?

Unlike the first two liars, the "protector liar" does not usually have a character disorder. He does not resort to dishonesty in order to save face or to win his wife's admiration. Usually his lying bothers him. But he feels telling the lies is worth it, because he wants to spare her the anxiety of everyday disappointments and uncertainties. He realizes she needs security, and he seeks to create it for her by painting a picture of a calm sea at a time when the waters are actually somewhat choppy.

The problem with all this is that his wife remains unaware of the pressure he feels. When the pressures of life make him irritable or moody, she finds it hard to understand. What happens, too, if his strategy backfires and he cannot pay back the secret loan as soon as he had hoped? Then his wife has to face a much larger and more alarming problem suddenly, with no warning whatsoever. I have seen clients whose husbands had kept the truth from them until the day the sheriff arrived at their door with the eviction notice. The false sense of security created by a "protector liar" husband with lies and misrepresentations can be shattered in a few seconds and do almost irreparable harm to a trusting marriage relationship.

How Little White Lies Empty Love Banks

It's obvious that being discovered in a lie about financial disaster can cause a minus-four withdrawal from the husband's account in a wife's Love Bank. But a man's "little white lies" about his feelings and attitudes about his wife can also cause withdrawals from *her* account in *his* Love Bank.

Suppose a wife feels concerned about being overweight. Her husband is even more concerned, but he decides it would do no good to tell her how disappointed he feels. Instead, he tells her she looks great.

Well, she thinks, *maybe a few extra pounds aren't so bad after all.* So she loses no weight, in fact she continues to gain. Her husband grows increasingly displeased with her unattractive figure, but bites his tongue. This time the Love Bank shoe is on the other foot. Daily withdrawals come out of *his wife's* account in his Love Bank, and she never becomes aware of them until the day he finally lets a cutting remark about her weight slip out, when it costs him a hefty withdrawal from his account in her Love Bank.

The husband who lies to "protect" his wife is often guilty of the worst sort of chauvinism. I have counseled many men over the years who believed their wives would fall apart if they told them the truth. This kind of man views his wife as an emotional basket case, incapable of coping with reality. Many men tend to make this assumption about women in general, sometimes because it feeds their own sense of superiority.

When a man lies to protect his wife he may also be saying she has little control over her habits and cannot readily change her behavior.

This kind of thinking reflects a low opinion of the character of women—another common attitude among men. Granted, some women reinforce these false assumptions because it serves their own purposes. They reason, *If I can get what I want out of Harry by looking like a helpless idiot now and then, why not?*

The "why not?" is easily answered. Whenever a woman uses helplessness or other manipulative behavior, she does not build her Love Bank account with her husband; slowly but steadily she empties it. Her behavior may feed her husband's false stereotype about "helpless women," but it cannot build his respect for her.

Subtly—or not so subtly—treating your wife as though she were emotionally unstable becomes a self-fulfilling prophecy. It is a great way to drive her a little bit crazy.

But when a husband tells his wife the truth, he builds her emotional stability. By always being truthful he tells her he knows she can handle it and can change when she must. The truth demolishes false impressions and illusions. Life becomes more predictable and rational because now she can understand her husband's behavior. The truth may be painful at times (and he should strive to deal gently with the truth), but truth does not drive a woman crazy. On the contrary, a woman feels in control, because now she knows what she needs to do to change the situation.

A husband does his wife no favors when he tells "protective" lies to make her feel secure and loved. Eventually exactly the opposite happens. A husband must present himself to his wife as he is. Then she can adjust, negotiate, and draw closer to him.

Does Privacy Have Its Place?

Many people ask me, "When you say I have to be so open with my spouse, aren't you taking away all my privacy?"

If by *privacy* that person means keeping part of himself or herself hidden, I hold firm to my conviction that this word has no place between a husband and wife. Many—colleagues and clients alike—disagree, but I have seen too many marital disasters follow the compromise of my principle. Although you may find it threatening to think your spouse might have the right to read your mail or go through your purse, I believe this kind of openness is indispensable for a healthy marriage. Let me show you how it might work.

When I "protect my privacy," it makes me less transparent to my wife. Joyce is the one person who needs to know me best, and I need to provide her with all the information—including the warts. Not only must I answer her questions truthfully, but I must avoid "lies of silence" and readily volunteer information as well. In other words, I must share myself with her in every way possible.

Over the years Joyce and I have worked out a little signal that we give each other when we feel the need for total honesty. We sometimes like to tease, but situations come up when we need to know exactly "where the other is at." When we have this need, we simply say, "On your word?" Whenever I hear Joyce use that phrase, I know she wants transparent honesty, not game playing or evasions.

Every married couple needs to work out a similar signal. Without the assurance that a spouse is on his or her word, a marriage limps along and eventually staggers right into trouble. As I counsel couples with troubled marriages I seldom find they have been totally honest with each other. For this reason, I usually see the husband and wife separately, especially at first. A spouse is far more apt to be honest with me when we are alone in the counseling room, for at least two reasons: (1) He or she feels an internal pressure to let the truth out to someone, and (2) they are paying for the time with me and want me to understand the problem as quickly as possible.

As each spouse "comes clean" with me I often get a clearer picture of both of them than they have of each other. For years they have wandered around blindly in the smoke screens each has laid down for the other. When they talk to me, they have no need for a smoke screen, and the real problem or issue starts to emerge.

All of Us Have Our Problems

One very valuable tool I use to get a clearer picture of people is S. R. Hathaway and J. C. McKinley's *Minnesota Multiphasic Personality Inventory* (MMPI), published by the University of Minnesota, a standard personality test psychologists have used for many years. The MMPI has an assortment of "scales" that help identify personal predispositions toward certain traits. Scoring high on any of these scales doesn't prove you have a problem, but it suggests that you may. The psychologist needs further evidence to support or refute the existence of a problem. For example, a person who scores high on the 1 scale is likely to be something of a hypochondriac. I am high on the 1 scale myself, but you probably wouldn't detect my hypochondriacal tendencies if you saw me only when I felt relaxed. When I'm under pressure, my "hypochondria" starts to show, because then I complain and carry on about my health more than many people would in similar circumstances. Joyce likes to remind me how I panic whenever I think I am sick, or when I experience emotional pressure. She's right. Normally, I do fine, but under pressure, my problem comes out. The significance of this "pressure principle" for marriages is obvious. A quick sketch of key traits revealed by the MMPI scales (0–9) includes the following:

0. Measures the tendency to be socially introverted, to avoid crowds, shyness.
1. Measures degree of concern about one's health and fear of death, debilitating disease, or that minor symptoms could turn into debilitating disease.
2. Measures depression, a feeling of hopelessness, a tendency to be pessimistic.
3. Measures suppression of feelings, the tendency to not be honest with yourself and others about why you feel the way you do.
4. Measures social alienation, the tendency to have problems with authority, and failure to consider others when meeting personal needs.
5. Measures masculinity and femininity, sensitivity to the needs of others, and willingness to care.
6. Measures sensitivity in close relationships, the tendency to idealize others, or prejudicial beliefs, both good and bad, about people.
7. Measures anxiety or fear, the tendency to be indecisive, perfectionistic, or guilt ridden.
8. Measures dissatisfaction with yourself, the tendency to be confused and undependable under stress.
9. Measures activity or energy level, reveals the tendency to be impulsive and overinvolved in too many things.

I include this mini-course in the MMPI only to show that in marriage a man or woman can have the kind of personality that may lead to difficulties when a couple tries to deal with conflict. If they want to solve conflicts successfully they need to know each other's emotional weaknesses that show up when they're under pressure. Dishonesty can be one of those weaknesses.

Using the ten scales I just described, a high 3 or 4 scale would indicate a problem with honesty and openness. Especially serious is the husband with a high 4. What could his wife expect? She'd probably find him self-serving, have trouble negotiating with him, and quickly learn that he becomes angry over small irritations. In addition, his lies and half-truths would show up his tendency toward self-centeredness. She might sum his character up by saying, "He thinks it's more important to have his own way than to tell the truth."

Obviously, if she rates high in the 6 scale, showing a tendency toward oversensitivity, and he is high in the 4 scale, marital discord is usually the outcome. While she must deal with her touchiness about getting hurt, he will have to try to learn to compensate for his predisposition toward dishonest, self-centered, and nonnegotiating behavior.

Does all this suggest you should rush right down to your local psychologist and get tested with the MMPI? I am biased, but I think you might find its results very useful. While you can't do much to change your personality, you can learn how to adjust to your spouse's personality. Tests like the MMPI only "prove" that we all have our personality quirks, weaknesses, and tendencies toward possible problems. That's why we must become as open and honest as possible with each other. We need to understand each other's problems so that we can accommodate and adapt to each other. Even if you discover your spouse scores high on the 4 scale, don't panic. Instead understand the nature of this weakness and learn to compensate for it.

How Mutual Honesty Can Rescue a Marriage

What happens when a marriage so lacks honesty and openness that it leads to the ultimate dishonesty of an affair? Can "coming clean" with your spouse help, or does it spell sure death for the relationship?

In a common scenario, I sit down to counsel with a husband who tells me, right up front, that he has been involved in a series of extramarital affairs. He has never told his wife about any of them, yet he feels "terribly guilty" about all of them.

As therapy proceeds, I suggest that he confess all this to his wife. With some fear and trepidation he does so, and she responds with predictable reactions: anger, anxiety, and finally depression. In time, however, she somehow gets through the shock and pain. Then their marriage can begin to be built on mutual honesty, perhaps for the first time.

When a couple deals with trying to survive an affair, I train them to become thoroughly candid with each other. They must conceal nothing of what they think or feel. Only through total openness can an honest relationship emerge. If they compromise at any point, it will only undermine the rebuilding process.

You may wonder if it is always wise for the straying spouse to confess his sins to his wife. In my experience, having the straying mate confess has never been the primary cause of a divorce. Some couples do go on to get a divorce because of the affair, but not because they have finally spoken honestly with each other. Instead quite commonly the betrayed mate—be it husband or wife—emerges from the initial shock of learning about the affair willing to examine and consider ways to resolve the marriage's problems. A lot depends on the therapeutic environment provided for the couple. The counselor must create an atmosphere that motivates the couple to discuss solutions for their real problems after the affair has been uncovered and exposed.

Once the dishonesty has been revealed, I make a special effort to help the couple to see the situation clearly. They have experienced a needed purging that provides them with their only opportunity to make a stable and lasting marriage. Now I must give them guidelines for restoring trust.

A husband with a history of lying may insist that his confession of the affair by itself proves he has reformed. He may want his wife to begin to trust him again immediately. But here I insist otherwise. You cannot turn on trust like a light switch. Rather, numerous experiences through which a person proves himself trustworthy build it. In a situation such as a confessed affair, I strongly recommend that a husband provide daily information to his wife, which she can easily check for accuracy.

I suggest to the man who has lied to his wife that he must write down a copy of his schedule for her to see every day. If the schedule changes through the day, he should try his best to notify her immediately. She should be able to call some of the places he has listed on his schedule in order to verify his presence. Usually they can handle this process of verification in a way that avoids any embarrassment to either husband or wife.

I often get flak from the husband about having to provide this kind of schedule. He often complains about legalism, childish rule keeping, and he says, "All this checking will only prove she doesn't trust me after all."

But that's just the point: She doesn't.

In response I simply comment that a well-organized person plans his schedule. Why should he be reluctant to share it with his wife? A wife should feel free to call her husband any time during the day, even in relationships that exhibit no problem with trust.

The procedure I've outlined sometimes takes years. Gradually, however, the wife finds through repeated verification that her husband is being honest with her. Then and only then can she begin to trust him to the point where she need not do any more checking up.

The typical woman needs the ability to communicate with her husband any time of the day or night in order to sustain this feeling of openness and honesty. Most women will not abuse this privilege by calling their husbands out of important meetings or otherwise interrupting them at work. However the wife must know that she *can* call if she wants to, and she believes that, when she calls, her trust in her husband is confirmed. In my book *Love Busters* I describe in greater detail how to build an honest relationship. I encourage you to read the chapter "Dishonesty" to gain further insight.

In twenty-five years of counseling I have never discovered the perfect marriage. Each partner has faults and weaknesses of one kind or another: a tendency toward depression; low ego strength; the tendency to crack under pressure; irresponsibility; tendencies toward hypochondria, oversensitivity, or perfectionism. The list could go on and on. However no marriage can survive two things: lack of honesty and lack of cooperation.

When honesty and cooperation exist in a marriage, you have a couple who is willing to share and to build together. They do not need to be secretive or "private." Neither wishes to lie and shade the truth to "protect" the spouse. When you build your marriage on trust, you experience a joyful willingness to share all personal feelings with the one you have chosen for a life partner.

According to Harley's Fifth Law:

> Honesty is the best
> marriage insurance policy.

In closing, I should reemphasize that a woman *needs* to trust her husband. Whatever advantage a man may gain in being secretive, closed, or even dishonest, he wins it at the expense of his wife's security and marital fulfillment. She must come to find him predictable; a blending of her mind with his should exist so that she can "read his mind." When a woman reaches that level of trust, she is able to love her husband more fully.

Questions for Him

1. On a scale of one to ten (with ten being totally honest), how honest are you with your wife? (How would she rate you on this scale?)
2. In what areas is it hardest to be "totally" honest and open with your wife? Why is it hard? How well does she handle it when you are candid about sensitive issues?
3. Do you agree or disagree with the contention that there should be no privacy in your marriage—that is, neither one of you should keep certain parts of yourselves from the other? Try putting your reasons for agreeing or disagreeing on paper.

Questions for Her

1. In your personal hierarchy of needs, how essential is being able to trust your husband? Do you agree that it is one of your five basic needs in marriage? Why or why not?
2. Has your husband ever lied to you in any way in order to protect you? If so, how did this make you feel?
3. In what areas, if any, do you wish your husband were more open and honest with you?

To Consider Together

1. Discuss your respective answers to the above questions. It will be a good test of how open and honest your marriage really is.

2. If you do not have an "on your word" signal already worked out, why not do it right now? What could you say to each other when you want to send the message that you need total honesty?

3. Go over the ten scales of the Minnesota Multiphasic Personality Inventory together. Do you see any tendencies that either one of you might have when you're under stress? Discuss the value in taking the MMPI together. You can usually find a psychologist who will do it for about seventy-five dollars.

4. Read chapter 6 "Dishonesty" in *Love Busters* together. What type of honesty needs the most improvement in your marriage?

8

HE NEEDS
A GOOD-LOOKING WIFE

AN ATTRACTIVE SPOUSE

At twenty-six and 190 pounds, Nancy seldom had dates—four in the last two years to be exact and no calls back after the first one. Her prospects for marriage seemed bleak, to say the least. Even though she had a charming personality and many interests, few men wanted to date her.

One day, Nancy decided she had to make a change. She wanted to marry, and she was tired of her job. *If I had someone to take care of me,* she thought, *I could quit the job and stay home all day. I'd like that.* As her first tactic in achieving that goal Nancy enrolled in an exercise program, went on a diet, and lost sixty pounds. Next she bought some new clothes that nicely accentuated her slender figure. A new hairdo and appropriate makeup completed the transformation.

With sixty pounds gone and the other improvements, Nancy became a real knockout. Now she had dates right and left, but she had not forgotten her goal—a husband. About eight months later, when Harold proposed, she said yes. She had achieved her goal with great speed.

When I counseled Nancy and Harold about five years later, I started by speaking to them separately. Harold told me, "The first thing she did after we were married was to quit her job. Then she stayed home, eating like mad all day. She blew up like a balloon—she's gained about a hundred pounds since we've been married."

"Have you said anything about her weight?" I asked.

"Yes, many times. In fact it's a sore point between us. But she just says, 'I want you to love me for who I am. If you'd love me and accept me unconditionally, then I could easily lose the weight.' I'm getting fed up," Harold continued. "I don't know *where* to turn. I don't believe in divorce, but I can't handle this, and something has to happen."

As we continued to talk, I could see Harold faced a real dilemma. Reared in a conservative church, he held strong convictions about marriage being a commitment for life, but whereas he had once looked forward to a happy future with a wife everyone seemed to admire, now life with Nancy seemed like a prison sentence. Marriage to this woman had hardly lived up to his expectations. Where had he gone wrong?

Next I talked to Nancy to get her side. She told me about her self-improvement program to get dates and a husband. Nancy had never told Harold that she had once weighed so much or that she didn't think she could keep the weight off after marriage. For her, dieting had been an agony, and even keeping slim was too great a sacrifice if it was for life. When she married Harold, she thought he would love her regardless of her weight, and she could go back to being fat and happy. So when he told her he was leaving if she didn't lose weight, she felt he was being unfair.

Things didn't seem fair to Harold, either. He had married someone physically appealing and assumed she'd stay that way. Nancy had thought that once Harold got to know and love her, her weight would no longer matter to him. But she was wrong.

Granted, some men do not care about physical appearance. Their wives can be overweight or underweight; it makes no difference. They have other emotional needs that are far more important than the need for an attractive spouse. But Nancy had not married one of these men. In fact, she had married a man for whom physical appearance was at the very top of his list. He needed an attractive wife.

Some women also have a need for an attractive husband. Many wives I've counseled have given their husbands the ultimate threat: You either lose weight or our marriage is over. One woman I counseled would not live with her husband until he lost fifty pounds.

If a person considers the need for an attractive spouse as the most important emotional need, physical appearance is serious business in that marriage. In Harold and Nancy's marriage, it was that serious.

Nancy listened intently as I explained that a marriage commitment means meeting the needs of your mate. She wanted Harold to earn a good living, be affectionate to her, talk with her often, and so on, but she wasn't holding up her end of the bargain.

"What do you mean, not holding up my end?" she snapped. "I cook good meals. I keep the house clean. I'm affectionate . . ."

"All that is good, but you're missing something," I explained. "Your physical attractiveness is very important to your husband. This isn't some quirk or whim. It's something he needs *very* badly. The beautiful woman he married hides under all that excess weight. By taking care of your body, you take care of your husband."

Nancy didn't quite hear me at first. She persisted in arguing, "Harold should love me as I am!"

"You want to be loved for who you are and not for what you do," I said. "We all do. But you didn't decide to marry your husband for who he is, but rather for what he did. If he had not met any of your emotional needs when you dated him, you would not have even considered him as a life partner. And if after you were married, he stopped meeting your needs, your feelings for him would have changed considerably. Your love would have simply faded away."

Many men think affection is a trivial need. Many women think sex is trivial. Some men and women think admiration is trivial. But none of these things are trivial to those who need them. Nancy couldn't see that physical appearance was not a trivial need. She wanted to believe that it was Harold's shallow sense of values that was the culprit. If he would grow up and be more mature, he would look beyond her appearance.

But we kept at it, and Nancy finally decided to lose weight. She didn't want to risk living without Harold and she knew deep down inside that it would be healthier for her as well. She enrolled in an exercise program, went on a diet, and lost forty pounds in three months. Once Harold saw she meant business, he joined her in the exercise program.

Nancy wanted to lose all the weight she'd gained since their wedding and she stuck to her exercise and diet. Once she got down to a desirable weight, Harold liked it, and she did, too. It greatly improved her feeling of self-esteem, and her attractiveness was the most important contribution she could make to her husband's happiness.

Many women (and men) have a problem like Nancy's, though it may be less severe. After they marry, they start to put on weight or dress less becomingly, figuring that their spouse loves them, so what they look like doesn't matter. For some people, especially husbands, nothing could be further from the truth.

Why All the Fuss about Looking Good?

People often challenge me when I list an attractive mate as one of the most important emotional needs. Surely, I'm told, men should have more maturity and higher values than to hold physical attractiveness up as an ideal. Shouldn't we be looking beyond the surface and into more meaningful human characteristics, such as honesty, trust, and caring? Besides, what if a woman simply doesn't have the equipment?

Beauty, of course, is in the eye of the beholder, and I am not encouraging a wife to try to look like a beauty queen. I simply mean that she should try to look the way her husband likes her to look. She should resemble the woman he married.

Does that mean a woman must stay eternally young? Of course not, but getting old is not an excuse for gaining weight and dressing like a bag lady. This is exactly what Nancy did, and it got so bad that she and Harold wound up coming to see me for help. Fortunately, under all the weight, Nancy had a determination to achieve her goals. Her story ended happily, but many do not. I have counseled other wives (and husbands) who refused to change. At best, this kind of marriage limps along. Often a husband is tempted to turn to women whom he finds more attractive.

If your husband tells you that your loss of weight would meet one of his most important emotional needs, you must decide if you care enough about your husband to meet his emotional need.

When She Looks Good, He Feels Good

A man with a need for an attractive spouse feels good whenever he looks at his attractive wife. In fact, that's what emotional needs are all about. When one of his emotional needs is met he feels fulfilled, and when it's not met he feels frustrated. It may sound immature or superficial, but I've found that most men have a need for an attractive wife. They do not appreciate a woman for her inner qualities alone. They also appreciate the way she looks.

Do most women have the same need for attractiveness in their husbands? No. They may want their husband to look decent, but most women do not rank an attractive spouse among their top five emotional needs. Women often fall in love with men who are overweight, homely, or sloppy dressers because these men know how to meet their most important emotional needs, such as the needs of affection, conversation, and financial support.

I remember an overweight, balding man who was twenty years older than his extremely pretty wife. Nonetheless, she was crazy about him and they shared a very active sex life. Why? What did she see in him? That's just the point. Instead of looking at him, she looked *within* him and found a warm and sensitive man, kind and generous, who loved her as deeply as she loved him. To her he was "rather nice looking."

Was she more mature than her husband, who was admittedly attracted by her appearance? No. She simply had different emotional needs. For her, physical attractiveness did not do as much for her as it did for him. She put effort into making herself look good because she knew it would make him happy. In return, he put effort into meeting her needs for affection, conversation, and financial support.

Any woman can enhance her attractiveness to her husband. There are plenty of books, videos, diet programs, and other products designed to help women (and men) shape up, dress with style, color their hair properly, and so forth. As I counsel women every week, I observe five major areas that are particularly important in staying or becoming attractive. Let's give them a quick survey.

The "Secret" to Weight Control

Every year several more best-sellers appear offering the latest "foolproof" diet or weight control plan. Here's mine, Harley's Third Corollary:

Balance your intake of calories with the proper amount of exercise.

I'm sorry I can't sound more sensational, effortless, or intriguing, but there is no "secret" to weight and figure control. It takes discipline, and that's been known for centuries.

I counsel many women who just don't believe me. They keep hoping for some revolutionary new gimmick that will solve their weight problem with little or no effort, or they crash diet and soon gain it all back. Then they crash again and again. Sooner or later they give up, fatter than ever.

The truth is that weight control programs work only when they are a way of life, based on the facts of life. All bodies, including female ones, are machines that burn fuel. When the body takes in too much fuel and doesn't burn it off, it stores the fuel in the form of fat. So if you want to avoid getting fat, you must burn all the fuel your body takes in. To lose weight, you must burn even more fuel.

Fuel, of course, is what you eat, and you burn it with exercise. You burn some of it by just sitting around, but it burns much faster with exercise. If you exercise often, you can afford to eat more because you're burning more fuel. From my perspective, however, it's much easier to eat less than it is to exercise more.

Yes, I know, you think you are addicted to food. But so is everybody—we all die of hunger without it. Hunger is a normal reaction to weight loss because our bodies are programmed to prevent weight loss. But that doesn't mean you can't eat less—it simply means you will be hungry while you're doing it.

You can eat lots of fruit and vegetables. Keep your refrigerator full of them. Snack on carrots until your skin turns orange (just kidding). Keep your intake of sugar and fat to a minimum. If you are tempted to binge on something with lots of calories (ice cream, for example), don't even buy it. That may be the only way to avoid being out of control. Your kids and your husband may complain, but they'll be as healthy as you.

Aerobic exercise will help you lose even more of the extra pounds, while keeping your heart and lungs healthy. All it takes is enough exercise to increase your heart rate to 60 to 70 percent of its maximum for about 30 minutes every other day. (To find your maximum heart rate, subtract your age from 220; then to find your best aerobic heart rate for your age, multiply your maximum heart rate by .70.)

Joyce and I share the same diet program, and we also exercise with each other whenever possible. We encourage each other in weight control. Both of us come from families where there has been a tendency to gain weight in later years, and we have made an agreement with each other to avoid that outcome.

If you have agreed to lose weight, and keep it off, you must create a new lifestyle around diet and exercise, and your spouse should be a part of it. It may mean that he will avoid foods that are not on your diet and join you in an exercise program. When both of you are committed to this new lifestyle, the chances that it will succeed are greatly increased.

Use Makeup to Your Best Advantage

Rose came into my office looking more like a clown than a well-made-up woman. Although she might have had some attractive features, they lay buried beneath a mass of colors vying for attention. Although obviously she had tried hard to make herself attractive, something had gone wrong. She hadn't used the makeup to her advantage.

Cosmetics have been around since the ancient Egyptian times, and with our modern multi-billion-dollar cosmetic industry no woman has the excuse that help is not available. Most women who use no makeup or use it inappropriately simply lack the initiative to get the help they need.

Some women have never applied makeup and do not understand the basic techniques. As in Rose's case, I sometimes step in where angels fear to tread and suggest that she might seek professional advice. Some cosmetic studios or large department stores provide free consultations that can help a woman start. Much depends on the knowledge of the person who gives the consultation, but many can give good results. Many women's magazines also publish articles that will help achieve the same goal.

I have seen many women make dramatic improvements in their appearance. These changes, in single women, are almost always followed by greater attention—and often dates—by single men. With married women, their husbands appreciate and encourage the change if their wives have done it for them. Be certain that in addition to being something *you* like, your husband also finds the cosmetic changes attractive. Keep in mind that your objective is meeting *his* need for your physical attractiveness.

Get a Hairstyle He Likes

Hairstyle and color are another sensitive area for women. Yearly they spend billions on dyes, rinses, shampoos, permanents, sets, and cuts. My question is, why and for whom?

If a wife spends all that time and money to please her husband, and to achieve something she finds comfortable, well and good. But if she lets some hairdresser talk her into something she knows her husband won't like, she has begun to work against herself—and her marriage. A certain hair-color manufacturer excuses the higher prices of his product by telling the woman, "You're worth it." More to the point, your husband is worth it. If he doesn't like a certain hairstyle and color, abandon it. In fact, consult with him ahead of time and get his opinion before ever getting a different style or coloring. After all, the whole idea is to be attractive to him.

Or is it? Some women object to this idea. They insist on the right to please themselves, or they argue that having to please their husbands in such a way seems unfair and even degrading.

I don't encourage women to meekly accept a hairstyle that makes them miserable. Certainly they need to enjoy their own looks and feel a sense of attractiveness. If a husband likes something his wife can't tolerate, negotiation is in order. Among the many hairstyles available, I'm certain they can find one on which they can agree.

Hairstyles, like everything else, can create deposits or withdrawals in her husband's Love Bank. If a wife understands her husband's need for an attractive mate, she will work with him to achieve that goal. Chances are great—in my experience—that she will find that her husband is quite reasonable and has fairly good taste.

Clothes Showcase the Woman

The old adage tells us, "Clothes make the man," but in our society, clothes showcase the woman. That showcase can enhance and flatter—or do something far less than that. As with cosmetics and hairstyle, the same principle applies: Dress to be attractive to your husband.

Fashions come and go, and in certain years clothing styles range from silly to disastrous. Despite the insistence of some clothes designers to be eternally creative, one rule still seems to prevail: When women's clothing becomes unappealing to most men, it does not stay popular very long.

A woman should pay as much, if not more, attention to her choice of nightgown or pajamas as she does to what she wears in public. When she dresses for bed, she dresses strictly for her husband. Wearing old and bedraggled night clothes, curlers, and "goop" on your face will not put points in the Love Bank. Wearing a worn-out nightgown to bed because "nobody will see it" misses an important point: One very special and important person does see it, so why not wear something attractive? Your husband will certainly appreciate it.

What about Personal Hygiene?

To be honest, I've hardly ever counseled a woman who needed help with her personal hygiene, but I've helped many men with this problem. Since the need for an attractive spouse is sometimes a wife's need, hygiene is a subject that should be addressed in this chapter.

Kent was a very successful farmer—he was worth millions. When he asked Jessica to marry him, all she could think about was his millions. He was a decent man but, having been single for the better part of his adult life, had paid little attention to his appearance. Jessica thought she could overlook his outward appearance and love him for his inner qualities—and his money. After they were married, however, she found his appearance turned her off.

When they came for their first appointment, Kent complained that Jessica refused to make love to him. She came up with every excuse, and he finally thought a counselor might help.

"I just can't have sex with him," she explained. "When I married him, I thought he would be more appealing to me, but it's getting worse. He'll probably divorce me, but I just can't do it."

When Kent came into the office, his body odor just about knocked me over! He had been chewing tobacco and his teeth were caked with residue. His hair was a mess, and his clothes looked like he'd slept in them. I had counseled many men who had trouble keeping themselves clean, but Kent was beyond anything I could have imagined.

"She doesn't like sex," was his explanation for their problem. I had a different theory.

"I think I can help you," I replied. "But you'll have to do everything I recommend. Within a few weeks I think your problem will be solved."

I gave him this assignment:

1. Take a shower every morning and evening.
2. With Jessica's help, buy a new wardrobe of clothes. Let Jessica pick out clothes for you to wear each day. Never wear anything you've worn the day before unless it has been washed.
3. Go to a dentist and have your teeth cleaned. Never chew tobacco in Jessica's presence and brush your teeth before being with her.
4. Comb your hair and shave every morning before breakfast.

Fulfilling this assignment was quite a commitment for Kent. He was used to going weeks without a shower. He wore the same pants and shirt day after day and he hadn't been to a dentist since he was a teenager. But he agreed to it, believing me when I said it would help his sexual relationship with Jessica.

Then I gave Jessica her assignment: Shop with Kent for clothes, pick out something for him to wear every day, and see to it that the clothes are clean. I also asked her if she would be willing to make love to him every day for just one week after he followed through on his assignment.

A deal was struck and Kent was off to the dentist and clothing store. He kept his part of the bargain and Jessica kept hers. After he had clean teeth, clean clothes, and a clean body, Jessica made love to him once a day for a week.

At their next appointment, I could hardly recognize Kent. What a transformation! And they were holding hands in the waiting room. All on their own, without my counsel, they had made a long-term agreement. She would make love to him if he would keep himself clean. Their sexual problems were over.

I'm sure they didn't make love every day from then on, but they were both satisfied with their new sexual compatibility. Kent had learned a very important lesson about Jessica. His physical appearance, especially his smell, was important to her sexually. At first she wanted to believe that outward appearances were not important, that she should love him in spite of his appearance. But the changes he made in his personal hygiene proved that her need for an attractive spouse was greater than she had been willing to admit.

The hygiene problems of most men are not as extreme as Kent's, but lesser problems can still have a devastating effect on wives, especially while making love. A woman wants to be physically close to the man she loves, especially if he looks and smells good.

Being Attractive Meets a Need

For those of you who are still unconvinced that physical attractiveness is a worthy objective, consider what it means to be physically attractive. It simply means that your appearance makes someone feel good. You meet an emotional need by the way you look. People can be attractive in many ways. Those with attractive personalities may also meet an emotional need, but they usually deposit love units with the quality of their conversation or affection, rather than their appearance. In fact, whenever someone meets any of our emotional needs, we consider that person attractive. If physical attractiveness meets an emotional need of your spouse, why ignore it? Why not deposit love units whenever you have a chance?

For some, like Nancy at the beginning of this chapter, the prospect of becoming physically attractive seems completely out of reach. In some cases these women have fallen for the lie that some women are born attractive while others are not. But they discover the truth of Harley's Fourth Corollary:

> Attractiveness is what you do
> with what you have.

Every woman would benefit from evaluating each aspect of the image she projects—her posture, hairstyle, clothing, gestures, makeup, weight, and so forth. She should ask her husband for his honest appraisal and, if possible, consult professionals or trustworthy friends.

The woman then should decide where change is needed and set real-istic goals for making those changes. For some, the changes might be completed in a week, while for others it could take years. But in the end, the makeover would have such significance that it would be life-changing—for the better.

Lydia, a client who suffered from depression, dramatically demon-strated how a woman can profit from an improved appearance. This exceptionally bright and charming woman wanted dates with men who were truly on a par with her, but she had not given her appearance the attention it needed. I reminded her how important appearance is to most men. Granted, it was not one of her emotional needs—she could not have cared less how the men she dated looked. But it was likely that the man of her dreams would have a need for a wife who was physically attrac-tive, and if she wanted to attract him, she would have to meet this need.

Her metamorphosis took six months to accomplish. At the end of that time, Lydia was a stunningly attractive woman. Men that she already knew and liked started dating her. Her depression disappeared entirely, and she no longer needed my services.

When I saw Lydia for the last time, I reminded her not to make the same mistake that Nancy had made—shaping up to attract a man and then letting herself go after marriage. Lydia knew that the changes she had made to attract a husband would have to be permanent because the emotional need she could meet by being attractive would continue to be there after marriage.

If you know how to make your spouse feel good, doesn't it make sense to go ahead and do it—whenever you can?

A wife's attractiveness is often a vital ingredient to the success of her marriage, and any wife who ignores this notion—for whatever rea-sons—risks disaster. This is true for some men as well. The changes in appearance I've witnessed in my clients have not only met spouses' needs but have also made my clients feel much better about them-selves. The changes have made them more successful in business and have improved their health. It's one of those efforts that pays dividends in ways that go far beyond the marriage itself.

When a woman sees the response of her husband to her improved appearance, she knows that she's made the right decision because it has met one of his deep and basic needs. Her account in his Love Bank will get a substantial deposit every time he sees her.

Questions for Her

1. Do I take my husband's need for me to be attractive seriously? If not, why not?
2. Does my husband really like the way I look most of the time? Do I?
3. How much care do I take about the way I look? How is my figure? Do I use cosmetics to good advantage? Do I change my hairstyles from time to time to please my husband by giving him a little variety in the way I look?

Questions for Him

1. Am I willing to own up to this as one of *my* most basic needs in my marriage? If not, why not?
2. Has my wife's appearance declined since our wedding? Do I really like the way she looks, or do I just say I do?
3. If my wife told me she was willing to change anything she could about her physical appearance, what would I ask her to change? Why?
4. How does my physical appearance affect my wife? Does she like it? Do I get lazy about the way I look?

To Consider Together

1. Sit down with your collection of photographs—especially those from the days when you were dating and from your wedding day. Compare those with the way you look today. Do you need to make some changes? How?
2. Share your answers to the above questions with each other. Be respectful but honest.

9

S H E   N E E D S
E N O U G H   M O N E Y
T O   L I V E   C O M F O R T A B L Y

FINANCIAL SUPPORT

Sandra had been raised comfortably in an upper-middle-class American home. She attended the state university where she majored in art, history—and George. They married while still in school.

George finished his undergraduate work and also earned a master's degree in fine arts. But once he was out of school, he could find no work that utilized his training. He tried to move into the world of commercial art, but the competition was fierce. Two years after graduation, he had still not found full-time work. He kept very busy with his painting and drawing, but his income was poor and unpredictable. During the first six years of their marriage, his jobs or assignments never lasted longer than six months.

Sandra, consequently, found herself working full-time as a receptionist to help make ends meet. She wanted to have children, but their finances prevented it. They lived in a modest apartment. Little money was on hand for extras, and they could afford only one inexpensive car.

Sandra knew several young executives at work who had started to climb the ladder of success. They all looked terrific to Sandra, dressed handsomely in one-thousand-dollar suits. Some were already earning incomes several times higher than George's would ever be.

Alan was also attracted to her. On several occasions she had helped him make sales by her skillful handling of customers on the telephone and in the lobby. That had motivated him to work more closely with her, and from time to time he would stop by her desk just to talk. The more he got to know her, the more he liked her.

During those conversations, Alan often heard Sandra say things like, "I feel so bad for George. He's so good at what he does, but it's hard for an artist to find a steady job." One day she broke down and started crying.

"Sandra!" His voice conveyed more compassion than alarm.

"I don't think George will ever earn much," she sobbed. "We'll never have anything."

"It's probably none of my business, but George has a good thing going," Alan suggested. "He can spend all day enjoying art while you're here supporting him. If he hadn't married you, he'd be working like the rest of us. I don't think he's being fair to you."

That started Sandra thinking. *George is using me!* she thought. *He's doing what he enjoys at my expense. If he cared about me, he'd give up his art work for a profession that could support us.* She became increasingly resentful about how trapped she was.

As time went by, Sandra and Alan became good friends. She found herself sitting and talking sales with Alan, first at her desk at odd moments, then at coffee breaks, and finally at lunch almost every day. He reminded Sandra of her father who was also a businessman—ambitious and prosperous. The more she came to know Alan, the more she felt it had been a mistake to have married George.

By predictable stages, the friendship grew into an affair. The weekend George had gone out of town to interview for a part-time teaching position, Alan invited Sandra to join him on his boat. That was the first of many times they made love.

The job didn't come through, but it started her thinking that someday she might be forced to move away from Alan so George could find a job somewhere. Or worse yet, George might discover her affair. To avoid those and other unpleasant prospects, she filed for divorce. A year later she married Alan.

Do Women Marry Men for Their Money?

Humorous anecdotes abound on women who marry men for their money, but my counseling experience has taught me not to treat this tendency as a joke. In truth a woman *does* marry a man for his money— at least she wants him to earn enough money to support himself.

I can recall talking to a woman who had a problem very similar to Sandra's. Her own marriage was intensely unhappy due to her husband's low income, but she insisted she would never "stoop to divorce" to resolve the problem.

"George is loyal and affectionate. I'd never be so selfish and uncaring as to leave him just because he doesn't make enough money."

"Oh," I replied. "Do you always feel that way?"

"Of course I do! Leaving a man who doesn't make enough money is a low-down, selfish thing to do." Alice seemed to know her mind, and convinced me that she would stick it out. Two weeks later, she missed her appointment with me, because she had filed for divorce and felt too ashamed to tell me about it. After the divorce was finalized, she married a man who earned considerably more money than her former husband.

Why did Alice make such loud protests against "stooping to divorce," when in the end she did not really have that strong commitment to marriage? Actually she didn't exhibit very unusual behavior. Often I counsel people who become what I call "verbally rigid" just before they crack. I believe Alice's inconsistent actions resulted from a struggle deep within her, between her values and her need for financial support. The incredibly powerful need to have enough money won over all her commitment and good intentions.

123

Married Women Often Resent *Having* to Work

Most men are willing to marry a woman who expects to be financially supported throughout life. But there aren't many women who would marry men they would need to support. Certainly most women would help support a husband through schooling that would prepare him for a vocation he enjoys. But when schooling is complete, the same women expect their husbands to find jobs.

Still, the difference in perspectives here goes beyond women expecting men to work while men remain open to the idea of their wives not working. Most wives do not only expect their husbands to work, they also expect them to earn enough to support their families.

Time after time I've been told by married women that they resent *having* to work. The women I talk to usually want a choice between following a career and being a homemaker—or possibly they want a combination of the two. They often want to be homemakers in their younger years, while their children are small. Later, when the children have grown, they often want to develop careers outside the home.

However, hard reality for many women today dictates that they must work to help make ends meet even when their children are small. Their husbands simply can't seem to handle the basic monthly bills on their own.

I strongly disagree with the materialistic trend that has forced women into the work force simply to "keep up with the Joneses," not to mention just to keep up with the bank and the credit-card bills. Many couples set a standard of living for themselves far higher than they need to be happy. If they would simply reduce their standards of living to a point of comfort, many could avoid husbands working long hours and wives pressured to earn a paycheck. Sometimes this single adjustment will give women the choice of career or homemaking that means so much to them.

Please understand I'm not against women who want careers and I don't oppose women who choose a career early in life. My daughter who is married with two small children earned a Ph.D. and is a licensed psychologist. I am proud of her achievement, and she is happy with her dual role as homemaker and psychologist. And so is her husband.

I wish, rather, to stress the principle that many women need to have the *choice* of whether or not to work once they have children. If they *do* choose a career, the money they earn should not have to be spent on basic support of the family. To put it all very simply, many families need to learn how to live on what a husband can earn in a normal work week.

If a couple can "bite the bullet" and lower an unrealistic standard of living, that action frees the husband to set realistic economic objectives regarding the family's basic financial needs. But as long as their wives keep working so that together they can finance the big house, big cars, and everyone's credit-card habit, where is the incentive to cut back?

I realize what I say will not be popular with many couples. Many will simply write me off as unrealistic. Don't I know that today a couple simply cannot live on one salary? No, I really don't know that, as I will explain later in this chapter. In fact, I know a family *can* live on one salary, and I will show you how it can be done. Right here I simply want to emphasize that there are many women whose need for financial support is deep and should be treated seriously. Most men don't have this need. In fact a husband rarely feels good when his wife supports him financially. If his salary pays the bills, he usually feels quite content if she earns little or nothing. By contrast, I have met very few women who sincerely feel content with a husband who earned little or nothing.

Some well-intentioned people, in the guise of advocating women's rights, encourage all women to develop a career, because they see employment as a right and privilege. However they fail to consider that a woman also has a right and privilege to be a homemaker and full-time mother. Those who argue that women do better to choose a career sometimes fail to understand their needs as mothers. I believe that women should have the choice of homemaking or career. When that choice is made for them by their husbands, women's advocates, or anyone else, it deprives many of them of marital fulfillment.

A Budget Is a Necessary Good

Every family must come to grips with what it can afford. Some couples look on budgets as a "necessary evil." I like to call a budget a "necessary good," and I recommend it to almost every couple I counsel. I have yet to meet a couple who sometimes didn't want to buy more than they could afford.

A budget helps you discover what a certain quality of life really costs. To more fully understand the quality of life you can afford, I recommend three budgets: One to describe what you *need*, one to describe what you *want*, and one to describe what you can *afford*.

The *needs budget* should include the monthly cost of meeting the necessities of your life, items you would be uncomfortable without.

The *wants budget* includes the cost of meeting all your needs and wants—things that bring special pleasure to your life. It should be realistic, however: No mansions or chauffeur-driven limos if these lie totally out of your price range.

The *affordable budget* begins with your income and should first include the cost of meeting your most important needs. If there's money left over when the cost of meeting all your needs is covered, your most important wants are then included in this budget until your expenses match your income.

To put these budgets in the context of need for financial support, I recommend that only the husband's income be used in the needs budget. In other words, if his income is sufficient to meet the needs of the family, by definition he's met the need for financial support. It may actually be covering some of the wants as well. Without these budgets, his success in meeting this need may not be obvious to his wife.

Both the husband's and wife's incomes are included in the affordable budget so that it's clear that the wife's income is helping the family improve its quality of life beyond their basic needs. Some women want to work for the challenges of a career; for others it's to escape from the children. But regardless of the reason, if her husband's income supports her basic needs, she's not working to support herself or her family. And she may decide that she'll have a higher quality of life by *not* working as much. She may not have as much money, but she has more time with her family. I've been amazed by the number of women who feel much better toward their husbands when his income actually goes to pay for her needs and those of the children. The Financial Support Inventory in appendix C will help you create a needs budget, wants budget, and affordable budget.

Can He Earn More?

But what happens when his income is not sufficient to pay for needs budget expenses? I have already admitted that lowering the standard of living will be a very distasteful option for many women. Resentful as they might be, they often prefer to work rather than lower their basic quality of life.

I've met countless couples caught in this trap. He works as hard as he can, coming home tired every night. But his paycheck just won't go far enough. His wife faces the impossible choice of being unhappy working to make up the difference or being unhappy putting up with an intolerable quality of life. Her Love Bank is draining. *How much longer can I put up with it?* she wonders.

I sympathize with the man trapped in this situation. He does the best he can yet cannot meet his wife's emotional need for financial support. Isn't there an answer to this kind of impasse? He must somehow increase his income without sacrificing time with his family. He can try to obtain a raise in pay, a job change that pays more, or he may need to go to the trouble of a career change. The following story illustrates how one couple solved this problem.

When Sean and Mindy came to me for counseling, Sean's career had reached a plateau. He had advanced about as far as he could with that company. I saw Mindy first, and she broke into tears. "I suppose I shouldn't feel this way, but I am losing respect for Sean. He can't earn enough to pay our bills, and now he wants me to go back to work to make up the difference. With the children so young, I just don't want to do that."

"What about cutting back on expenses?" I asked.

"As far as I'm concerned we're at the bare minimum now. I suppose we couldn't afford a bigger house, but now we're into it. We could never get along without a second car. We just live too far out to leave me home alone without some kind of transportation."

I could see that talking to Mindy about lowering her quality of life was pointless, so I pulled out the only other card in my hand.

"Perhaps Sean could earn quite a bit more if he finished his education—I believe you said he had two years left. Would you be willing to go to work to help him?"

"Well, I suppose I could—just so it wouldn't be forever," Mindy replied. "I'll talk to Sean and see what he thinks."

Within a few weeks Sean and Mindy had it worked out. She had found a full-time job, and his company had allowed him to take a part-time position so he could attend college and finish his degree.

Their new plan saved their marriage. Mindy was pleased to see Sean trying to improve his income-producing potential, and she did not mind the sacrifice, because she knew it wouldn't be permanent. Ironically enough, Mindy loved her job so much that she continued working even after Sean had completed school and earned enough to support her. In the end she gained respect for her husband and a valued career for herself.

If a husband's income is insufficient, he should improve his job skills. While training for this new job, the family may temporarily lower its standard of living, his wife may go to work, or perhaps both adjustments will be made. I have found that women are usually willing to lower their quality of life and go to work to help support the family if it is a *temporary* solution to a financial crisis. In fact, making this kind of temporary sacrifice can often prove to be a powerful builder of rapport and affection in a marriage. When a husband and wife work together toward a common goal, their spheres of interests are much more likely to overlap, and their conversations will become more interesting to each other. In short, they become a winning team, and players on a winning team usually like and respect one another.

How to Live on $1,000 per Month

Having counseled so many couples like Sean and Mindy, I've become aware of how little it costs to be happy. As a short-term measure, while education is being completed, couples learn to cut their costs to the bone. Once the changes are made, they're often amazed at how satisfied they are living on a shoestring.

When I first met Sarah and Jim, they had set themselves adrift and seemed headed for the financial rocks.

Both worked full-time, but things they bought with their dual income gave them little pleasure. They became addicted to drugs and alcohol, abandoned their moral values, and seemed destined to self-destruct.

When they came to see me, I convinced them they both needed a new direction in life and that a college education was a good place to find that direction. They had only one problem: They were used to living on their combined incomes of $9,000 a month, and they could never earn that much and attend school, too.

I suggested a radical solution. "Have you ever lived on one thousand dollars a month?" I asked.

They looked at each other and started to laugh. "No one *can* live on one thousand dollars a month," Jim responded.

"Oh, on the contrary, most people in the world live on less than half that much. You might find it interesting to experiment and see how the rest of the world does it."

The two of them left my office that day still chuckling and shaking their heads, but I had planted the seed. It took them several weeks to make the decision, and I am certain they thought the experiment would become something like joining VISTA or the Peace Corps. Nonetheless, we worked out the following monthly budget:

Housing and utilities	$ 400
Groceries	$ 200
Clothes	$ 100
Miscellaneous and emergencies	$ 300
	$1,000

They rented a single room with an area for cooking, near the university they attended. Because they had sold their cars, they rode the bus or biked to school and work. They bought nourishing but inexpensive food. All their clothing purchases were at thrift shops. They already had acquired their furniture. The money from the sale of their cars and unneeded possessions went into savings.

Each of them worked only fifteen hours a week to earn the $1,000 they needed. They actually earned more once in a while, but agreed not to spend more. Now they could not afford drugs or alcohol and had to overcome their habits. Funding for their education came almost completely from grants. When they completed their education, they still had money in their savings account.

I witnessed the change in their lives. Because the credits in their Love Banks had risen, they were undeniably happy. Their marriage, about to end in divorce when I first saw them, now flourished. This change took place *while* they lived on $1,000 a month.

It's possible to live on much less than we do. I am not trying to convince you that you should live on $1,000 a month. Surely families with children would face serious problems. But almost any family *can* live comfortably on less than they presently spend. I simply want you to open up to the idea that many people think they need things they may not really need. They sometimes become their own worst enemies. They sacrifice the fulfillment of their marital need for financial support by creating a standard of living they cannot meet. Men sometimes work themselves to an early grave providing for living standards that their families can do without. Sometimes we may measure the cost of high living standards in the loss of life's most valuable treasures.

Together you may prove the truth of Harley's Fifth Corollary:

> **When it comes to money
> and marriage,
> less may be more.**

Questions for Him

1. On a scale from −4 (very unhappy) to +4 (very happy), how happy are you in your present job?
2. When you first married did you think your wife would expect you to support her financially? Did you expect her to work?
3. Do you think your wife is satisfied with the money you can presently earn working a normal work week?
4. Have you recently considered retraining so that you could qualify for a job that earns more money? Would cutting household expenses accomplish the same objective?
5. Would your wife willingly cut some household costs? Would she be just as happy after those cuts were made?

Questions for Her

1. On a scale of −4 (very insecure) to +4 (very secure), how secure do you feel with the financial support your husband presently provides?
2. Have you thought much about your husband's income and how it affects your standard of living? If so, how do you feel about it?

3. Would you feel comfortable sharing with him any negative feelings you may have about your level of income? Have you shared them in the past?

4. Are you willing to reduce your standard of living so that you can be supported by the income of your husband? Do you want to be able to choose between a career and raising a family full-time?

To Consider Together

1. What is your current standard of living? Do you both feel happy with it? Do you really have enough money to meet it?

2. Use the form Financial Support Inventory found in appendix C to create a needs budget, a wants budget, and an affordable budget.

3. Do you need to make some changes? If so, which plan would best suit your needs? Begin to decide together how to implement the changes you need.

10

H E   N E E D S
P E A C E   A N D   Q U I E T

DOMESTIC SUPPORT

Phil was a prosperous young bachelor. His job paid well. Because he had made a substantial down payment, his car payments were low, and his apartment was pleasant, nicely furnished, and well situated. He had dated a number of women before he met Charlene. But she turned out to be different—special. They became best friends, and after about eight months of dating, he asked her to marry him.

The wedding took place in October. At first they lived in his apartment. But that was just to give them time to finish accumulating money to put down on a house. Because Charlene had a good job, too, they had no trouble pooling their resources in order to become homeowners.

The next summer they found the place they wanted, and they moved by September. Phil relished many of the responsibilities of owning a home—caring for the yard, making repairs, installing new fixtures, and so forth.

Everything went well until their first child arrived. Then Charlene decided to cut back to part-time work. That cut their income at a time when their expenses escalated. Phil took a second job to compensate for the loss of Charlene's income. He found himself working twelve-hour days, first as manager of his department, then as a part-time book-keeper for another company.

At the end of five years, Phil and Charlene had three children. Phil still worked two jobs, but coming home from his second job, he found the demand greater than ever. Charlene still needed things fixed and sought help with the children. The lawn still needed mowing, and Charlene began to complain that their two-bedroom house was not large enough for the family.

Life, once so pleasant for Phil, rapidly became intolerable. He tried to escape by watching television and reading the newspaper. But that didn't work well, because Charlene could still bother him and make him get up and help around the house. Next he started staying after quitting time and hanging around with some of his coworkers. But that only aroused Charlene's ire. She felt hurt and angry when he wasn't coming home in time to help.

Not long after that, Phil found Janet, a fellow worker he could talk to and relax with. Within a year, he and Janet became involved in an affair. When I interviewed Phil, I learned that Janet was the single parent of six children. Phil would stop by her place about midnight, after he got off his second job. Janet's kids would be in bed, and a delicious steak dinner awaited him—along with the royal treatment. After dinner, they made love and went to sleep. Janet geared everything to Phil's relaxation and pleasure.

This pattern persisted for months, with Phil never going back home. His wife, both furious and desperate, attempted to win him back by going to his office once in a while in the middle of the day to have sex with him. But she did not make much progress, because she felt too furious to give Phil the warmth and affection he got from Janet. In addition, the stress she underwent became so great that it seriously affected her health.

When Phil and I talked, I told him, "If you were single, you would never look twice at Janet. She's overweight, homely, and has six kids! She's not at all your type."

"But I love her," he protested. "I've never loved a woman so much in my whole life."

Eventually Charlene couldn't take it anymore and as soon as she left Phil, his affair with Janet fell apart. I knew it would, because Janet had provided a service in competition with Charlene. When that competition with Charlene no longer existed, much of Janet's motivation was lost. Besides, Janet had provided a degree of service no woman would want to provide for a husband in a marital relationship. Janet thought she had Phil hooked and decided that now *she* deserved some of the royal treatment. The midnight steak dinners ceased, and Janet started making demands on Phil and giving him a taste of what being around her six kids felt like.

Phil backed out. He stopped seeing Janet, and after months of missing his family, he went back to Charlene, willing to work together toward the goal of reuniting. Their relationship improved tremendously once she could understand Phil's need for what I call "domestic support." I also worked with Phil and Charlene on their budget and helped them cut living expenses so Phil could work only one job. It's not that Phil wasn't glad to help out at home—in fact, with only one job to take care of, he picked up on a lot of chores Charlene had felt he neglected. At the same time, however, Phil desperately needed to feel that his wife handled the household and the children in an organized and efficient way. Charlene had been unwilling to assume the responsibilities of the home and had instead overemphasized her demands that Phil share the load. With all the hours Phil had to spend earning a living, Charlene's demand had seemed overwhelming. That caused him to go off the deep end in his relationship with Janet.

Domestic Bliss: A Man's Fantasy

Unmet emotional needs often trigger fantasies, and the need for domestic support is no exception. Men often fantasize about a home life free of stress and worry. After work each day, his wife greets him lovingly at the door and his well-behaved children are also glad to see him. He enters the comfort of a well-maintained home as his wife urges him to relax before taking part in dinner, the aroma of which he can already smell wafting through the air.

Conversation at dinner is enjoyable and free of conflict. Later the family goes out together for an early evening stroll, and he returns to put the children to bed with no hassle or fuss. Then he and his wife relax and talk together, watch a little television, and go to bed to make love, all at a reasonable hour.

Some wives may chuckle as they read the above scenario, but I assure you that if there is a wide gap between the reality of your home life and this fantasy, your marriage may be in serious trouble. A revolution in male attitudes in housework is supposed to have taken place, with men pitching in to take an equal share of the household chores. But this revolution has not necessarily changed their emotional needs. Many of the men I counsel still tell me in private that they need domestic support as much as ever.

If behavior is any measure of attitude change, I don't see much change in the way men really feel about housework. They are not helping around the house much more than they did a hundred years ago. They may talk a lot about how unfair it is to expect women to do all the housework, but when it comes to actually doing it, their wives know that it's mostly talk.

How to Create a Fair Division of Labor

With the advent of so many dual career marriages, the division of domestic responsibilities has become a major source of marital conflict. Changes in our cultural values have contributed greatly to the problem, because there is now almost unanimous agreement that both a husband and wife should share these responsibilities, particularly child care. But change in behavior has not kept pace with the change in values.

Traditionally, wives have assumed most household and child-care responsibilities, while husbands have taken the responsibility of providing income for the family. When couples could afford it, housekeepers and nannies lived in the home to take the burden of those responsibilities off the shoulders of the wife.

But today, at least in America, there are fewer live-in housekeepers and nannies, and women are much more committed to work outside of the home. That combination of factors makes husbands the most obvious resource to fill the gap. While men are changing the diapers, wielding the mop, and tending the stove more often than ever before, it usually isn't nearly enough. In dual-career marriages, men, on average do less than half as much child care and housework as their working wives.

As most women have figured out by now, men are not very motivated to do housekeeping. Many husbands think that any effort to help with household responsibilities represents a monumental sacrifice. But from the wife's perspective, he is simply doing a small part of his fair share of the work. In many of these marriages, the husband demands that the wife do most of the work, and the wife demands that the husband do it. Neither feels it is their responsibility.

Domestic responsibilities are a time bomb in many marriages. Marriage usually begins with a willingness of both spouses to share them. Newlyweds commonly wash dishes together, make the bed together, and divide many household tasks. The groom welcomes the help he gets from his wife because, prior to marriage, he'd been doing it all alone as a bachelor. At this point in marriage, neither of them regard domestic responsibilities as an important marital issue. But the time bomb is ticking.

When does it explode? It's when the children arrive! Children create huge needs, both a greater need for income and greater domestic responsibilities. The previous division of labor is now obsolete. Both spouses must take on new responsibilities. Which ones should they take? In most modern marriages, both spouses opt for income, leaving the domestic responsibilities to whoever will volunteer. It's a recipe for disaster, at least for most working women, because they end up doing most of the housework and child care, resenting their husbands' lack of support.

If household responsibilities are given to whoever is in the mood to do them, nothing much will be done. If one spouse demands help from the other, that will also have an unsatisfactory outcome. But if assignment of these tasks can be mutually agreed upon by willing spouses that accept the responsibility, everything will run smoothly. I would like to propose to you a solution to your conflict. My solution will not only resolve your conflict, but it will meet the need for domestic support.

This solution will require you to do something that is essential in solving most conflicts: get organized. It means you must think through your problem carefully and systematically. You will need to write down your objectives and create solutions that take each other's feelings into account. While you may find all of this awkward and terribly "not you," there is no other way. Besides, when you're done, you may find it to be more comfortable than you anticipated.

Step 1: Identify Your Household Responsibilities

First, make a list of all of your household responsibilities including child care. The list should (1) name each responsibility, (2) briefly describe what must be done and when to accomplish it, (3) name the spouse that wants it accomplished, and (4) rate how important it is to that spouse (use a scale from 0–5, with 0 indicating no importance and 5 indicating most important).

Both spouses should work on this list, and it will take several days to cover the bases. You will add items each day as you find yourself accomplishing various tasks or wanting them accomplished.

Each time a task is added to the list and the work is described, the spouse wanting it done must be named along with their rating of the task's importance. But the other spouse must also consider to what extent he or she would want it accomplished. So the names and importance ratings of both spouses should eventually accompany each item.

Examples of items on the list are as follows:

Washing the breakfast dishes—clearing off the breakfast table every morning; washing, drying and putting away all the breakfast dishes and utensils that went into preparing breakfast—Becky (4); John (2).

Feeding the cat— put cat food and water in the cat's dishes at 8:00 a.m. and 5:00 p.m.— John (5); Becky (0).

When you have finished your list, both of you should be satisfied that it includes all of the housekeeping and child-care responsibilities that you share. You may have as many as a hundred items listed. Just this part of the exercise alone will help you understand what you're up against with regard to the work that you feel must be done.

Step 2: Assume Responsibility for Items That You Would Enjoy Doing or Prefer Yourself

Now make two new lists, one list titled "his responsibilities" and the other titled "her responsibilities." Then select items that you are willing to take full responsibility for all by yourself. These are tasks that you would enjoy doing, don't mind doing, or want to do yourself so they can be done a certain way. When you have added an item to one of the two new lists, cross it off the original list.

If both you and your spouse want to take responsibility for the same items, you can either take turns doing them, or arbitrarily divide them between the two of you. But you must approve each other's selections before they become your final responsibilities. If one of you does not feel that the other will perform the task well enough, you might give each other a trial period to demonstrate competence. Once you have taken responsibility for any item, your spouse should be able to hold you accountable for doing it according to his or her expectations.

Now you have three lists: (1) the husband's list of responsibilities, (2) the wife's list of responsibilities, and (3) the list of household responsibilities that are not yet assigned.

Step 3: Assign the Remaining Responsibilities to the One Wanting Each Done the Most

Assuming that all tasks you would not mind doing have been eliminated, we are left with those that would be unpleasant for either of you to perform. These are items that neither of you wants to do, but at least one of you thinks should be done.

It is at this point that you may choke on my recommendation. I suggest that these unpleasant responsibilities be assigned to the person who wants them done the most. It's a reasonable solution, since to do otherwise would force responsibility on the one who doesn't care about them.

Consider for a moment why you want the other person to do these unpleasant tasks for you. Even though you are the one who wants them done, you want the other person to relieve you of the pain you suffer when you do them. It other words, you want to enjoy the benefit of having them done, but you are not willing to suffer for it yourself. You would rather see your spouse suffer. You want to gain the benefits of having these unpleasant tasks accomplished at your spouse's expense.

You may argue that these tasks are not really what you want done, but rather what *should* be done. For example, you may say that they are for the benefit of your children. But when you use that argument, you imply that your spouse is such a slob and so out of touch that he or she doesn't even know or care what's right or what's best for the children.

While that may be precisely the way you feel, it's incredibly disrespectful. You are assuming that your view of the situation is superior to that of your spouse. You are trying to straighten him or her out. But I guarantee you that your argument will not be well received. Whenever you try to impose your way of thinking on your spouse, you make your spouse feel bad, which withdraws love units. And you usually won't win the argument! So why do it?

By following this procedure, you may decide to change your attitude about some of the responsibilities on your list. When you know that the only way to do something is to do it yourself, you may decide that it doesn't need to be done after all. In fact, you may find that what kept you convinced of its importance, was the notion that your spouse was supposed to do it.

So far, we have a fair division of labor, but we have not addressed the need for domestic support. So there is one more step in my plan that may not only make you feel much better about my solution, but it will help you meet one of your spouse's most important emotional needs.

Step 4: Meet the Need of Domestic Support by Assuming Responsibilities That Deposit the Most Love Units

Up to this point, the assignment of household responsibilities is fair. You are dividing responsibilities according to willingness and according to who benefits most with their accomplishment. But marriage takes you one step further. In marriage, you do things for each other because you care about each other's feelings, not just because you want them done yourself. And that can deposit carloads of love units if done the right way.

You may not be willing to take responsibility for a certain task because, quite frankly, you don't think it needs to be done. But if your spouse thinks it needs to be done, it may be an opportunity for you to meet his or her emotional need for domestic support.

To be sure that your effort is not wasted, both you and your spouse should add one more piece of information to your lists of tasks. Beside each task write a number indicating how many love units you think would be deposited if your spouse would do that task for you. Use a scale from 0–5 with 0 indicating that you would experience no pleasure and 5 indicating that you would experience maximum pleasure and would be eternally grateful.

If these ratings are accurate, it means that whenever you have completed a task that was rated a 4 or 5 by your spouse, you will be depositing many love units. In fact, for some spouses that rate domestic support as their most important emotional need, when someone completes these tasks, enough love units may be deposited to trigger the feeling of love.

Let me repeat a concept that is crucial to your marital happiness. If you and your spouse are in love with each other, you will have a happy marriage. If you are not in love you will feel cheated. So whatever it takes to trigger the feeling of being in love with each other is well worth the effort.

If cooking dinner or ironing shirts or picking up socks triggers the feeling of love in your spouse, why not do those things? In fact, if meeting any of the emotional needs that I've described in this book really does create the feeling of love, why would anyone resist doing it? It is not only an act of care, but is an act of supreme wisdom. By doing for each other what you appreciate most, you will have what few marriages have, the feeling of love throughout your entire lives.

But let me repeat another important concept. Don't waste your time on needs of lesser importance. Put your energy into what deposits the most love units, and ignore tasks that do nothing for your Love Bank.

Don't do housework or child care for your spouse if it is not appreciated. Remember, whatever's on your spouse's list is your spouse's responsibility, not yours. You help your spouse with these tasks for one and only one very important reason—to build your Love Bank balance. If your effort to relieve your spouse of a particular task really doesn't deposit love units, don't waste your time. Put your effort into another task that gives you more bang for the buck.

Your spouse's response to your help should prove whether or not love units are being deposited. If your spouse thanks you when you perform the task and expresses his or her appreciation with affection, you know you are on the right track. But if your spouse ignores you after performing one of these tasks, love units are not being deposited for some reason. In that case go back to your spouse's original list of tasks and pick something else to do that has a greater impact.

Just because you decide to help your spouse with one of his or her responsibilities does not make it your responsibility. In fact, that's a very important way to look at meeting emotional needs in general. If meeting any emotional need is viewed as a responsibility, then it is not appreciated as much when it's met. Only when the meeting of emotional needs is seen as a gift—as an act of care—does it have the maximum impact on the Love Bank. If either you or your spouse take the meeting of any emotional need for granted, it will tend to dilute its effect.

If your spouse sees a burdensome task as his or her responsibility and you perform that task, he or she will appreciate the help you give. On the other hand, if your spouse views it as your responsibility, then your efforts have much less impact. So the first three steps of my plan to meet your spouse's need for domestic support are crucial. Unless you establish a task as your spouse's responsibility, your efforts will tend to be taken for granted.

I must make one final point. If you suffer in an effort to meet your spouse's need for domestic support, you will never get into the habit of meeting that need. And deposits in your spouse's Love Bank will be offset by withdrawals in yours. So you must figure out a way to meet your spouse's need for domestic support without the loss of your own love units.

There are many ways to get things done, and you may not have considered the best possibilities. You and your spouse should discuss how the most burdensome responsibilities can be accomplished in ways that are not so burdensome. Maybe one of you would not mind doing one part of dinner preparation, and the other would not mind doing another part. Or maybe you would agree that going out to dinner is the ultimate solution to the problem (you still meet the need, without having to do the work).

There are certain household tasks that are so unpleasant for both spouses that hiring someone to do it is a reasonable alternative, especially when both spouses work full-time. Hiring a housekeeper once a week to do only the most unpleasant cleaning chores is money well spent. The same thing can be true of maintaining the yard. Having someone mow and trim the lawn can turn a burdensome Saturday into an opportunity to enjoy the day with the family.

On a related subject, be sure that you do not assign your children tasks that both you and your spouse find too unpleasant to shoulder. It doesn't build character to give your kids jobs that you hate to do; it builds resentment. If you want your children to help around the house, have them choose tasks from your list of household responsibilities that they would enjoy doing. Make lists for them, as well as for you and your spouse. There will be plenty to keep them busy.

To summarize, when creating a plan for division of household responsibilities, depositing the most love units and avoiding their withdrawal should be your guide. Assume household responsibilities that you enthusiastically accept or want accomplished more than your spouse does. Then, to meet your spouse's need for domestic support, perform some of the tasks on your spouse's list of responsibilities that will be appreciated the most. And do them in a way that doesn't withdraw love units from your own Love Bank.

This approach to the division of household responsibilities guarantees your mutual care, especially when you feel like being uncaring. It prevents you from trying to gain at your spouse's expense, and from trying to force your spouse into an unpleasant way of life with you. It points you in a direction that will give you both happiness, fulfillment, and best of all, the feeling of love for each other.

Questions for Her

1. Do you feel that your husband expects too much from you? Does he understand all the responsibilities you try to balance in a day?
2. How can you communicate to him your willingness to provide domestic support, but the difficulty you have fitting it in? Are you willing to eliminate some of your responsibilities to make room for domestic support?

Questions for Him

1. Have you felt pressure from your wife to help meet domestic tasks that you feel are her responsibility? How have you tried to communicate your feelings?
2. What affects your willingness to help with domestic responsibilities? What could your wife do to make your participation in these tasks easier?

To Consider Together

1. Discuss the ways you have burdened each other with responsibilities:
   a) With a standard of living that requires more time at work than you like.
   b) With children's activities that are more work than you anticipated.
   c) With church or volunteer work that takes time away from your family.
   d) With hobbies and recreational interests that take time and resources away from higher priorities.
2. If a need for domestic support has been identified, how do you plan to meet the need in a way that you can both enthusiastically agree? To help you with this plan, use the steps suggested in this chapter.

11

SHE NEEDS HIM
TO BE A GOOD FATHER

FAMILY COMMITMENT

Ann and Terry met in their early thirties. Neither of them had been married before, and both felt ready to settle down. Their relationship was very good, with one exception: Terry had no use for Ann's parents. Ann felt bad about this, but she knew other couples who had problems that seemed worse to her. She and Terry got along so well in every other area that she decided to try to live with the problem.

Maybe, in time, it will work itself out, she told herself.

Terry's eagerness to get away from Ann's family considerably dampened the wedding. She hardly had time to greet her relatives before her new husband whisked her away to the honeymoon trip.

During their first year of marriage Ann tried to interest Terry in her family get-togethers, but to no avail. She soon learned that he would have little to do with his own parents, much less spend time with hers.

The problem didn't "work itself out," in fact, as their two children arrived it got worse. When they were only babies, Ann wrote it off as a typical male attitude. *He'll be more interested when they get older*, she thought.

But Terry didn't become more interested. He had little time for them, and when they clamored for his attention, he became irritable. Ann finally quit hoping and admitted to herself that she had married a man who just wasn't family oriented. She worried about what would happen to the children—especially little Tommy, who really needed his dad.

Ann hated to admit it, but Terry's bachelor cousin, Drew, was a better father to her children than Terry. Drew visited regularly on holidays and over some weekends. He was so good with the kids they called him Uncle Drew. Drew eventually became their favorite baby-sitter, especially when Terry and Ann went away overnight. Drew's popularity with Ann's children left her ambivalent. While she could see Drew becoming their "father" in a sense, and that worried her, she also found comfort in knowing her children received the male supervision and companionship they needed so badly.

One day, when Ann shopped during the noon hour, she saw Drew. After a few moments of conversation, Drew said, "Look, why don't we get some lunch?"

"I'd love it!"

After they had placed their orders with the waiter, Drew asked, "Well, how are my kids?"

His tender concern brought tears to Ann's eyes. "I've never told you how I worry about them," she began. In a few minutes she had poured out all her fears and worries about Terry's lack of commitment to the family. She concluded by confessing, "Sometimes, Drew, I feel as if you act more like a parent to my children than Terry does."

Drew turned a bit red, but still had to smile. "You know I love those little guys as if they were my own." He reached across the table and held Ann's hand. "Look, I want to help. I'll start making a point to drop by more often to see them. In fact, how about if I take them to the county fair on Saturday?"

"That would be wonderful!" Ann beamed. "I might even come along myself."

Ann did go to the fair with Drew and the kids that Saturday. It began a steady pattern in which Drew earnestly sought to help compensate for his cousin's lack of commitment to his family. Terry did not seem to mind. He trusted Drew as a good friend as well as a member of the family.

Over the two years that followed that luncheon, Ann and Drew began to see more and more of each other. They met often for lunch in addition to sharing outings with the children.

Ann began to admit to herself that she needed Drew in her life. He supported her in what seemed to be her most important responsibility: the care and development of her children. Slowly, over the months, their friendship became an affair. She came to love him with greater intensity and passion than she had ever loved any man.

The conflict that developed in Ann was unbearable. On the one hand, she did not want their children to go through the pain of divorce and be separated from their true father; on the other hand, she could not bear raising her children without the support of a man she loved.

Ann struggled with her emotions until Terry discovered the affair. He felt hurt and angry that his own cousin would betray him. To avoid the wrath of Terry and the rest of his family, Drew moved to another state. Now Ann felt doubly devastated. Her lover was gone, and so was the man who had acted as a father to her children. Where would she go from here?

A Wife Needs a Strong Family Unit

Affairs like the one between Ann and Drew are not common, but they do happen. I have counseled several couples like Ann and Terry, and every situation repeatedly impresses on me the wife's strong need for a family unit. Despite the current trend among many young couples to avoid having children, I still believe that the vast majority of women have a powerful instinct to create a family. Above all, wives want their husbands to take a leadership role in this family and to commit themselves to the moral and educational development of their children. The ideal scenario for a wife is to marry a man whom she can look up to and respect and then have her children grow up to be like their father.

In the Bible Jewish parents were advised: "Train up a child in the way he should go, and when he is old he will not turn from it" (Prov. 22:6). Whatever their religious convictions may be, most of the wives I counsel have no trouble seeing the wisdom in the above words.

They also expect their husbands to play a key role in "training up the children."

Women seem to know instinctively what we psychologists have discovered in research and practice: A father has a profound influence on his children. My own father exerted a powerful influence on my educational and moral development. He may not have known it at the time, because I often disagreed with him on many issues. Upon reaching adulthood, however, I found myself leaning toward his views more often than not. This development of my own moral values was extremely important to my mother, and I am certain she gives him a great deal of credit for training me up in the way she wanted me to go.

In families where the father takes little interest in his children's development, the mother tries desperately to motivate him to change. She buys him books on parenting and leaves them in convenient places. She coaches him to attend seminars sponsored by the church or PTA. She may even ask him to talk with a family counselor in the hope that he can be inspired to greater interest and commitment. Her efforts usually meet with only partial success. More often she becomes frustrated by excuses, delays, and other unenthusiastic responses on her husband's part. Not uncommonly such a mother starts looking to other men in her family or circle of friends to meet her need. She believes the children have the need, but in reality the need is hers. She must have a man contributing to the well-being of her children. Sometimes a grandfather does the trick; other times a man like Drew appears and takes the place of the father with the children—and the place of the woman's husband as her lover.

What does a woman really mean when she says she wants her children to "have a good father"? Behind that remark lie expectations of responsibilities she wants him to fulfill. Ironically enough, they often conflict with his need for domestic support, which we considered in the last chapter. In order to deal with such a situation, the couple must achieve open communication in two important areas: time and training.

Parenting Takes Time—Lots of Time

In addition to giving his wife fifteen hours of undivided attention and spending about fifty hours making a living, a man also needs to devote time to his family. He can strengthen both his marriage and his ties with his children by developing what I call "Quality Family Time."

This is not to be confused with child-care efforts parents make to feed, clothe, and watch over children to keep them safe. Quality Family Time is when the family is together for the express purpose of teaching the children the value of cooperation and care for each other.

I recommend fifteen hours a week for Quality Family Time. At first those hours may seem impossible to find in your schedule. Perhaps your first week will only allow five hours for your family, but if you increase that by only one hour a week, in ten weeks you will find yourself right on target, with only minimal effort.

What should you plan on doing during these hours? Consider activities such as:

- Meals together as a family.
- Going out for walks and bike rides.
- Attending religious services.
- Conducting family meetings.
- Playing board games together.
- Attending sports events.
- Reading to the children before bedtime.
- Helping the children with financial planning.
- Family projects (be certain these are fun for the children and that they do not work on them alone).

Naturally your list will also include other things you enjoy. Every family has different priorities. Your aim is family togetherness; during this time encourage family members to help each other, showing cooperative spirit. Make it a time for fun with your children, not a time of drudgery. As your children realize Mom and Dad will spend time giving them undivided attention, they begin to look forward to the time.

If you have children under the age of twelve, you will find it fairly easy to motivate them to spend time with you in this way. Once they reach their teens, however, expect that they will begin to tax your ingenuity. Now they want to spend most of their time with their friends; your family begins to see less and less of them. To compensate, develop well-planned events aimed at teens; otherwise they will express their dissatisfaction clearly and with great vigor!

If your children have grown up with such family time, it should not be too hard to get them to continue the practice. That doesn't mean you will not be challenged by teens who have other plans; but with some more thought—and perhaps more expense—in your plans, you can develop something your teens will *agree* to continue.

Families beginning family time during the children's teen years may find the youngsters will not agree at all to such an arrangement. In cases where heated arguments occur between parents and children, so much harm may be done by these fights that I often recommend that the family forget about quality time together; they have simply, though sadly, lost that opportunity.

Most educators realize that children are easier to influence than teens or adults. Take a leaf from their book, and if your children are still young, make the most of your ability to mold them with quality moral standards and life principles that can benefit them for years. Keep in mind the goal of training your child "in the way he should go," with his future needs in mind. If you take family time seriously in their early growth stages, you will not find yourself in trouble later, because you ignored your youngsters in this key developmental stage.

Parenting Takes Training—Lots of Training

If you wish to parent your children well, you also need to face the fact that you will need some good training in this skill. No one automatically knows how to care for a child, no matter what the stereotypes may lead you to think.

While both men and women benefit from parenting classes, in my experience, men seem to need the training more. Mistakenly many may think of parenting as an instinct—you're born a bad or good parent, and you can't control the factors involved, they believe. Because they feel this way, they resist the training I recommend.

Terry, Ann's husband, didn't believe training would do him any good. Because he recognized the bad habits that made him a terrible father, he had avoided spending time with his children. Drew seemed to know what to do better than Terry did, so Terry let him take over. But no matter what happened, only Terry could be the real father. If only Terry had realized that he *could* learn the skills he needed! Just as with any skill, he could improve by reading good books on parenting or taking some classes. When he had become more expert, his children would have enjoyed his presence tremendously, and Terry would have felt more comfortable around them. As a grand prize, Terry would also have met one of his wife's important needs.

Hundreds of books on parenting appear on bookstore and library shelves each year. Look for books that show you some sensible ideas for improving your relationship with your children rather than seeking out those that advise you to control them. In the long run, you'll find such ideas more effective.

Countless seminars try to explain how to train children. If they stress the parent's respect for the child and show parents ways to improve communication, they, too, may help. I believe mutual respect and understanding form the foundation of an effective training system.

Parent-instruction manuals, books, and courses abound with information on everything from toilet training to enforcing bedtimes. But in regard to a woman's need for a good father for her children, far and away the most significant area any husband needs to work on is learning to discipline children properly. Even more important, he needs to learn how to work with his wife in disciplining children. Some guidelines for fathers follow:

1. Learn how to be consistent.

Many fathers make mistakes in consistency, and children don't take long to discover that the rules may depend on Daddy's mood. When he feels happy, they can do almost anything: run around the house, throw things, jump on the beds, yell at each other, and have a squirt-gun fight. When he comes home grumpy—watch out! Movement of any kind will be met with an angry outburst.

Children need to understand the differences in appropriate and inappropriate behavior. In inconsistent disciplining parents do not always see the same behavior as wrong—it only becomes wrong for Johnny to yell at the top of his lungs when Daddy needs to concentrate on something or doesn't feel up to par. Father, make rules, stick to them, and discipline your children consistently.

2. Learn how to punish properly.

While I oppose violence, I do not object to a parent's spanking a child. Children whose parents *never* spank them often run wild. Instead, use corporal punishment wisely, learning when it is appropriate and for what age. (Generally I recommend that parents phase out spanking by the time a child reaches age seven or eight.)

Noncorporal punishment also proves effective in many situations. But use it to help instead of hurt your child. Most commonly parents take away privileges—but they must be dealt with carefully. Some well-meaning parents have taken away some basic rights from older children, only to have their teens run away or even attempt suicide.

Don't forget the most effective method of discipline for some cases: rewards. Use them appropriately, making certain you don't "bribe" a child, instead of reward him. Children should not grow up expecting all good behavior to receive compensation. On the other hand, wisely considered rewards can often work to encourage a child to change his behavior, particularly in the case of a well-developed bad habit.

3. Learn how to reach agreement with your wife.

Men must see child training as a joint effort with their wives. If they can get away with it, children will make a "deal" with Mom to get around Dad. When a child wants a privilege, both Mom and Dad should consult in private and give an agreed-upon answer.

Reach agreement, too, on how you want to discipline your children. A joint opinion receives greater respect from children and carries more weight with them. When they know you made it together, children are less likely to challenge your decision.

In family after family I have witnessed children successfully manipulate one parent who favors them. Father favors Mary; Mother favors Joan. So Mary goes to Father for money, and he tries to give it to her without Mother knowing. When Joan finds out about it, she demands the same treatment. Mother tries to make Father give Joan the same amount of money, resulting in a deep wedge driven between husband and wife. To avoid this, all decisions *must* result from mutual agreement. If you cannot agree, take *no* action.

How husbands discipline their children greatly affects their Love Bank deposits in their wives' accounts. Women are very sensitive to inappropriate and overly harsh discipline. Often they react as if the punishment the man gives their children had been given to them, personally, and this incident results in Love Bank withdrawals. Therefore a man needs to be careful about reaching agreement with his wife before imposing a disciplinary solution. If the plan would hurt her, she needs the opportunity to modify it. She also needs to encourage her husband to implement a solution that builds her love for him. Then her Love Bank gains new deposits, reflecting the care he took for her feelings.

4. Learn how to interpret the rules.

Children need to understand *why* they should do this or that. Men especially should learn how to clearly and patiently explain the rules. Sometimes the conversation may go like this:

"Johnny, go upstairs and make your bed."

"Why?"

"Because we want you to grow up knowing how to keep yourself and your property neat and clean."

"Why?"

"Because being neat and clean makes the people you live with feel good and like living with you."

"Why?"

"Just go upstairs and make your bed *BECAUSE I SAID SO!*"

"Oh, okay."

You can easily understand the father's reaction to those seemingly endless questions, can't you? But the "because I said so" line doesn't benefit the child very much. When you feel frustrated, pulling out your parental muscle may work—you may get the child to take the appropriate action—but you may also have lost the opportunity to explain your rationale to the child. In situations such as these you can subtly but clearly communicate your moral, ethical, and personal values, if you patiently answer the *whys*.

5. Learn how to handle anger.

Men often feel tempted to use anger as a means of communicating displeasure. Some even resort to violent behavior and batter and bruise the child. Such sad reactions by parents do not work, and no child psychologist I have ever studied has recommended anger in any form as a tool for training a child. Control your anger *before* you discipline any child. By separating your emotion from the disciplinary action you will become a more effective parent.

Fatherhood Takes Commitment

Many men view this need for family commitment as a very demanding role—sometimes too demanding. Not only must they act as good husbands, providing their wives with affection, conversation, honesty, and financial support, now they must become good fathers, with the time and training that requires. Because they fear being overcome by all this, they may neglect the role of father, turning all the parenting over to their wives. By avoiding the role of father, a man loses his wife's respect and the Love Bank account loses out.

On the other hand, men who accept the challenge of good fathering report that they come away with increased marital fulfillment. Their effort comes back to them many times over in the admiration of their wives. As Harley's Ninth Law of Marriage says:

| The best husband is a good father. |

Seek out the books and courses that will make you a better father. Spend time with your children. You'll be glad you did!

Questions for Him

1. Have you committed yourself to your family? What does that mean in regard to quality family time? training in parenting skills?
2. Are you experiencing any problems with anger? punishment? consistency? agreement with your wife in child discipline?
3. Are you overcome with responsibilities? How have you tried to communicate your juggling act to your wife? Does she seem to understand?

4. Do you have a plan, which you and your wife have agreed upon, with which your problems of family commitment and parenting will be resolved over the next few months? If not, do you plan to get some help to resolve this problem?

Questions for Her

1. List some of the skills your husband has mastered in learning to raise your children.
2. List the skills you think he should develop in learning to raise your children.
3. How many hours do you spend each week in quality family time activities?
4. How have you tried to convince your husband that you need his commitment to the family? Can you think of a more effective method?
5. How have you tried to encourage your husband to spend time each week with the family? What would be a more effective method?
6. How have you tried to encourage your husband to educate himself in parenting skills? How can you do so more effectively?

To Consider Together

1. Do you have an agreement on how your children should be disciplined? If not, make some time to discuss this issue and come to a conclusion on what you both find fair.
2. Explain your moral values to each other. It will help you explain them to your children.
3. Subscribe to *Family Fun* magazine (1-800-289-4849) for a host of ways your family can enjoy quality family time.

12

H E N E E D S H E R
T O B E P R O U D O F H I M

ADMIRATION

"Oh, Charles, thank you." Louise's eyes lit up with excitement. "What a wonderful painting! No one ever gave me his own original artwork before. You have so much talent."

"I don't know about that, Louise. I've got a long way to go."

"You underestimate yourself, honey. You are good. I know enough about art to know that. You always do such fine work. You're a great artist, and I'm proud of you."

In Charles's and Louise's courtship days that would have been a typical snatch of conversation. She forever heaped praise on him, and it felt great. No one had ever complimented him that way before.

After the marriage, Louise's remarks gradually started to change. Charles, contented with his job in commercial design, seemed altogether too relaxed about his career to suit her. She wanted him to become a famous artist. As she began to feel convinced he would never develop his potential, Louise's words of admiration tapered off and finally ended altogether.

Meanwhile, at the studio, Charles found himself teamed more often with Linda. She showed a knack for layout and graphics, and together they came up with some winning displays. One day as they shared lunch Charles started to unburden himself to her. "You know, Linda, I think my wife is right. I haven't done much to develop my career in art. I'm too lazy."

"Lazy!" Linda protested. "How could she think that? Does she know how tough this business is? Why, I can't think of *anyone* your age who has gone farther than you as an artist. Your wife just doesn't understand what it takes. Besides, you're one of the nicest men I've ever met. She should feel lucky she married someone as wonderful as you."

Charles hardly knew what to say. "Thanks, Linda," he finally managed. "It's really kind of you to say that."

"It's not just kindness. I meant it."

Charles savored the compliment all day. Someone finally appreciated him for what he was right now, not for what he could become someday. It felt good to live up to someone's expectations for a change.

Not long after, Charles and Linda began their affair. When the president of their company found out about it, he referred Charles and Louise to me for marriage counseling. Louise learned how to express the admiration she already felt for her husband, instead of pressuring him to greater achievements.

Why This Male Need for Admiration?

One of the principles I taught Louise was that honest admiration is a great motivator for most men. When a woman tells a man she thinks he's wonderful, that inspires him to achieve more. He sees himself as capable of handling new responsibilities and perfecting skills far above those of his present level. That inspiration helps him prepare for the responsibilities of life.

Admiration not only motivates, it also rewards the husband's existing achievements. When she tells him that she appreciates him for what he has done, it gives him more satisfaction than he receives from his paycheck. A woman needs to appreciate her husband for what he already is, not for what he could become, if he lived up to her standards.

For some men—those with fragile self-images—admiration also helps them believe in themselves. Without it these men seem inherently more defensive about their shortcomings. Often they hate to see a counselor, because they do not want someone to be critical of them. They often come to me in the guise of "helping their wives with their emotional problems."

While criticism causes men to become defensive, admiration energizes and motivates them. A man expects—and needs—his wife to be his most enthusiastic fan. He draws confidence from her support and can usually achieve far more with her encouragement.

Self-Esteem Usually Begins at Home

Low self-esteem, one of the most common problems I help clients overcome, begins very early—in the home, during childhood. Most often the person with low opinions of himself has had friends and family who criticized and complained about his failings, and he has expected others to continue that critical pattern. In particular he expects his wife to pick up where his parents left off and continue to remind him of his shortcomings and failures.

In such cases I advise clients to reject these negative evaluations, and I encourage them to surround themselves with friends and relatives who see their value and accomplishments. Often such a change does the trick, and within weeks self-esteem improves measurably. An environment of carping and criticism is dangerous to your mental health. Those who support and encourage you bring out your true potential and spark your genius.

In my own life, I've seen the powerful effect of admiration through the blessing of an admiring grandmother. As a small child I vividly remember her telling me that I was a genius and more talented than anyone in the whole world. Although that somewhat misguided belief created some social problems for me in kindergarten, her attitude toward me also placed within me the seeds of confidence.

In high school a counselor once reviewed my grades and other test scores and concluded I could never succeed in college and should seriously consider skilled labor. Since my grandmother had thought otherwise, I went to college anyway, did much better than the counselor expected, and went on to earn a doctorate degree. Without my grandmother's admiring opinion, I might have agreed with my counselor and failed to gain the benefit of that education.

You've heard the saying, "Behind every great man is a great woman." I'd like to amend it to make Harley's Sixth Corollary:

> ## Behind every man should be an admiring wife.

Biographies of great men prove it, and lives of all men show it: A man simply thrives on a woman's admiration. To a great extent men owe gratitude to their wives for this kind of emotional support, for without it, their confidence—the major source of their success—erodes and eventually crumbles.

How Do You Show Admiration Honestly?

Before you begin heaping words of praise on your spouse, I need to give you a word of caution. Never fake your admiration. By simply saying flattering words to your husband, you can do more harm than good. To have any value, praise must genuinely reflect your feelings. For example, when my grandmother told me she thought I was brilliant, she honestly believed it, and her conviction convinced me.

I can hear a lot of wives saying to themselves, *That's all well and good, Dr. Harley, but what if your husband is a constant source of irritation? What if he always fouls things up? How can I learn to admire a man like that?*

These very important questions require thoughtful answers.

The first step in learning how to express admiration is to learn how to feel admiration. When you achieve that, you can express these feelings.

A Plan to Create Admiration

You need a plan to help you express true feelings of admiration. That means no word games, nothing phony, only true, honest feelings.

You've seen how the Love Bank works, how learning to meet each other's marital needs creates the feeling of love. Well, the process of creating the feeling of respect in a woman works in a very similar way. As a husband learns to meet his wife's five most important needs she finds herself responding with a natural and overflowing respect for him. Conversely, if a man does not meet these needs, she cannot in all honesty express the admiration he needs from her. Therefore her admiration depends on his ability to meet her basic marital needs.

Keeping this observation in mind, our plan must help a woman see to it that her marital needs are met.

Step 1: Identify characteristics that build and destroy admiration.

A wife must make two lists, the first describing the characteristics she admires in her husband, the second describing those that destroy her admiration. In both lists, she groups these items into the five basic need areas we have already considered for women. Where a characteristic falls out of the areas, she must try to name the need as best she can.

As an example we will look at a list that Rachel made that evaluates her husband, John.

Characteristics that I admire	Characteristics that destroy my admiration
AFFECTION	AFFECTION
1. Holds my hand when we're out together.	
2. Hugs me when he comes home from work.	
3. Sends me surprise cards and flowers.	
CONVERSATION	CONVERSATION
4. Talks to me about how his day went and how I spent mine.	1. When I feel upset, he buries himself in his work and won't talk to me.
5. Takes an interest in my daily activities and discusses them with me.	
FINANCIAL SUPPORT	FINANCIAL SUPPORT
6. Earns a good income to support me and our children.	
HONESTY AND OPENNESS	HONESTY AND OPENNESS
7. He always tells me where he has been and leaves numbers where I can reach him in an emergency.	2. When something bothers him, he denies it, even though I can tell he's upset.

Characteristics that I admire	Characteristics that destroy my admiration
FAMILY COMMITMENT	FAMILY COMMITMENT 3. He does not take enough time to be with me and our children together as a family. 4. He does not discipline the children, but leaves the training entirely to me. 5. He never shows any interest in our children's activities and never attends PTA meetings.

The example above shows that John must begin to meet his wife's need for family commitment before she will be able to admire him completely. Their difficulty with conversation may relate directly to his failure in family commitment: Rachel becomes upset with his lack of interest in the children, and he will not talk about it. Since he already feels overextended and has no time for the children's projects, he decides talking about it cannot help. When he can meet the need for family commitment, their conversation problems may disappear.

Step 2: Making a trade.

It is sometimes easier to resolve a marital problem when both husband and wife need to improve their ability to care for each other. You'll feel encouraged knowing you're not the only one who needs to make changes and that your spouse has to take some corrective action, too. So, from a practical standpoint, you will more successfully motivate your spouse to make changes in his behavior if you are willing to make a few alterations yourself; also, prepare yourself for a defensive reaction from him when he reads your list. With gentleness and patience you can prove to a man who would like to please you that he *will* succeed. Prove his fears wrong.

Once you have completed the first step and have listed your strong and weak areas, agree together to overcome the characteristics that destroy admiration for either of you. Ideally, your trade-off should include *all* items you've listed.

Several years ago Ben and Charlotte came to me for counseling, and I helped them make up such lists. Immediately their marital problems became apparent. Charlotte handed me twenty-four single-spaced pages of things her husband did that destroyed her respect for him. His list had only one item: She didn't admire him enough. In this marriage Charlotte had done a terrific job meeting his needs, and Ben had done an awful job of meeting hers. Because of his failure, Charlotte could not admire her husband. I was at a terrible disadvantage because I could not think of any trade. Eventually when I simply explained that he might lose her, Ben got the incentive to make some changes. Over the period of a year he worked on her grievances one at a time, until they were met. As he succeeded, her admiration also blossomed, and he eventually reported that she felt proud of him.

If you find yourself in a situation like Ben and Charlotte's and a trade-off is not possible because you are already meeting your husband's needs, explain that you have only your admiration to trade. If your husband will not work with you on that basis, you may need professional help to get him started.

Once you've made your trade (if possible) and are willing to work on your spouse's grievances, you move on to the next step.

Step 3: You can't change traits. You can change habits.

Now you need to change the way you think about people—your spouse in particular. We tend to classify people by traits or characteristics. Someone is pleasant or unpleasant, intelligent or stupid. A behavioral psychologist doesn't like to work with traits. He would rather work with habits. He'd tell you, "I can't teach you to be more pleasant, because *pleasant* isn't a habit, it's a trait. But I *can* teach you to smile more often and criticize people less, because those are habits, and we can change habits. Will that help?"

If you told a behaviorist, "I want to be thin," he'd reply, "I can't teach you how to be thin; that's a trait. I *can* teach you to eat less, because eating is a habit."

This just means that as long as you forget about traits and focus on habits, you can change the behavior of your spouse. Often, when we complain about our spouses, we look at their traits not their habits. Yet habits are usually what we really mean and we can do something about them. So your easiest solution will be to define your grievances in terms of habits—then you'll both have something you can measure and evaluate.

For example suppose you want your spouse to show greater family commitment. List specific habits you'd like him to learn:

Attend PTA meetings.
Spend fifteen hours each week in family activities.
Read to the children before they go to bed.

Your husband will have a goal to aim at with these habits, which he can learn, practice, and use as a measure for change. You'll both see the difference in his actions.

But be warned: While your spouse learns a habit, his attitude may not seem consistent with the new behavior. He may not feel "right" about the change. In most cases, however, once he develops the habit thoroughly, his attitude will begin to conform to the habit, and you'll have what you really wanted in the first place.

Now let's see how a behaviorist would help you learn those new habits.

Step 4: Learning new habits.

Most behaviorists use this fairly simple and straightforward technique to help people develop new habits:

1. Define the habit you want to create.
2. Plan the strategy you will use to develop that habit.
3. Follow the strategy.
4. Evaluate the strategy's effectiveness to see if behavior has changed.

Let's see how it worked for John and Rachel. When they made up their list, Rachel said that John's lack of interest in the activities of the children destroyed her admiration for him. After much thought, Rachel converted the characteristic "interest in the activities of the children" into a habit, "spending five hours each week working with the children in any of their activities." John accepted that challenge.

Once they identified the habit, John and Rachel could plan the strategy to help him learn it. They decided it would have three parts:

1. Sunday night at 7:00 he would ask the children what activities they planned that week.
2. For each child he would select an activity with which he could help.
3. He would set aside five hours to use for these activities.

Every strategy must include incentives for following the new habit and disincentives for falling back into old habits. Together John and Rachel planned that she would watch "Monday Night Football" with him when he spent the five hours with the children; if he failed to do so, he could not watch any sports on television that week.

One reason people don't learn habits is that they often just don't give it enough time. John and Rachel planned to leave their strategy in effect for five months, August through December.

Once they announced the plan to the children, they were off to a running start. For eight weeks straight John spent the time with the children. On the ninth week he slipped. He had many good reasons: He got sick and fell behind in his work; he had to repair the front door; and Rachel's sister dropped in for a two-day visit. Despite those good reasons, he could not watch sports for the next week, and Rachel didn't have to watch football either.

The rest of the program went as planned, and at the end of December they evaluated his new habit to see if their strategy had worked. The indications seemed good. Not only did he now spend five hours with the children in their activities, he had begun to plan new ones with them, where he could help them even more. He enjoyed being with them more than he liked "Monday Night Football"!

Prepare for Setbacks

When I work with couples on forming new habits, I warn them that they may find their first efforts disappointing. Their original plan may need several revisions before they reach the goal of a new habit. Naturally, if the problem had been easy to solve, they would not have required my professional help. Some problems may even seem difficult from a professional's viewpoint, but in the end, together we can usually resolve them.

You'll need patience and optimism in your efforts to improve each other's habits. You'll find, though, that even *progress* can make your marriage so much better that you'll begin to feel the admiration developing.

What Do I Do When I Begin to Admire Him?

Tell him, of course! However, that obvious answer is not always as easy as it seems. You may not have learned how to tell your husband you admire him. Just because you *feel* pride or admiration, you have not communicated it. Teach yourself to speak those words of praise, just as you have learned any other habit. Again, remember not to say something contrived or phony. Express honestly how you feel. At first that may seem awkward, but as your habit develops it will become smoother and more spontaneous. Then you'll have achieved your goal: the natural admiration he's always wanted from you.

Sometimes a woman fears expressing praise too soon, because her husband might stop working on behavior that has not yet become habitual. I advise her to communicate praise as soon as she feels even a *little* admiration—not as a reward for change (you can find other methods to use for that), but as a true expression of her feelings.

Remember that a man really *needs* appreciation. He thrives on it. Many men who come to me because they have had affairs stress that the admiration of their lovers acted as a warm spring breeze in comparison to the arctic cold of their wives' criticism. How can they resist? Don't make your husband go outside your marriage for approval; he needs the perspective your appreciation gives him. That does not mean you have to fake it with him and tell him you love something that drives you wild, but work with him on the needs you must both fulfill, setting up a strategy that builds admiration. You need to admire him as much as he needs your praise. Gently and patiently encourage your husband to meet your needs by telling him how much you like the changes you see.

Questions for Her

1. Has the expression of admiration toward your husband been a special problem for you? Has he ever asked you to be less critical of him or encouraged you to "count your blessings"?

2. Do you need to develop a feeling of admiration or simply the habit of expressing your admiration?

3. Make the list of changes you would like in your husband. Next separate out traits, converting them to habits. Now divide the list into essential changes and unessential changes. If your husband made these essential changes, do you think you would be able to show him the admiration he needs?

Questions for Him

1. Are you very aware of your need for admiration? Some men never give it a thought and don't think they need it. What evidence might there be in your life that you have a deep and basic need for praise from your wife?

2. How have you tried to communicate the need of admiration to her? How has she responded?

3. What do you think of the plan suggested in this chapter? How might you modify it to make it more applicable to your marriage?

4. Make the list of changes you would like in your wife. Separate out traits, converting them to habits. Now divide your list into essential changes and unessential changes. Are you willing to make the changes your wife will suggest to you, if she makes the changes that you would like her to make?

To Consider Together

1. Develop strategies for changing the habits you've identified. Set a time limit on the strategies and plan to reevaluate them to see if they work.

2. Discuss the disadvantages of your criticism toward each other. How can you encourage each other to change, without being critical?

13

How to Survive an Affair

I am often asked, "How do you help people survive an affair? What do you tell a couple when this actually happens to them?"

My approach to treating affairs centers on two words: be *gentle*, but *firm*.

People caught in the web of an affair need tender loving care—especially the betrayed spouse. At the same time, if you discover your spouse in an affair, do not resort to hand wringing or hysterics. If you want to save your marriage, it is time for action.

Step 1: Do You Want to Survive?

First, you must ask yourself if you truly want to survive the storm. Quite possibly your marriage has been in serious trouble for a long time, whether or not you've realized it. One or both of you had unmet basic needs, which gave the affair a chance to develop. The wronged party will feel tempted to point the accusing finger and may, almost always prematurely and foolishly, simply want to call the marriage quits. With those who come to me for counseling, I try to point out that the straying spouse is not the only guilty party. Affairs start because Love Bank accounts have slowly emptied. Distasteful as it may be, the victim of an affair has to ask, *How did my account get that low in my spouse's Love Bank? What need was I failing to meet?*

Step 2: Don't Put Up with It

Second, don't put up with the affair for another minute. You may have failed to meet certain needs for your spouse, but that doesn't mean he (or she) is not responsible for the extremely destructive behavior. As I said in chapter 1, marriage is an exclusive relationship in which two become one and should stay one. Three is definitely a crowd.

My counseling files include a surprising number of cases where women actually put up with their husband's affair, in order to stay married. Often people who have strong religious convictions tell me: "My church doesn't allow divorce." "God wants us to stay married. The Bible clearly teaches that divorce is a sin."

I sympathize with these viewpoints because they are very similar to my own values and convictions. At the same time people must understand that once an affair has begun, the marriage has already been breached. What God has joined together, some man (or woman) has put asunder. If you want to put it back together, you have to take definite action. I urge wives in particular to take a hard, independent line and be willing to separate from their husbands temporarily until they can solve this matter together. Whatever they do, they must make it clear to the straying spouse that they will not put up with this.

Step 3: Know What to Expect

Most affairs do not lead to divorce—they lead to reconciliation. But during the months or years that lead from an affair to reconciliation, the whole process can inflict almost unbearable pain on you. If you prepare yourself for what is to come, you'll not only suffer less, but your marriage has a better chance of surviving.

One of the best ways to prepare yourself is to know what to expect. Having witnessed so many affairs, I have seen some common threads run through most of them. One of the most common threads is the spouse's resistance to give up the lover.

I use an iron-clad rule that the straying spouse must stop making any contact with his or her lover immediately and never see or talk to that person again. To explain why my rule is so rigid and extreme, I tell clients that I view an affair as an addiction. An alcoholic, for example, must abstain from all alcohol if he/she expects to control the addictive behavior. As with alcohol, the temptation to return to a lover must be controlled one day at a time. The best way for a person to become disentangled in an affair is to avoid all contact with his/her lover.

Time and again I've watched people in affairs fail to make drastic and decisive breaks with their lovers. They manage to "go on the wagon" for a while, but inevitably they find their way back to their lover's arms. It seems that when it comes to this one person, they exhibit incredibly flawed judgment and almost irresistible force draws them.

The permanent effect of an affair cannot be ignored. The straying spouse rarely falls out of love with the ex-lover. The feelings lie dormant ready to snap back as soon as they're reacquainted. The Love Bank account of the ex-lover remains high because few opportunities for withdrawal exist. Only an unpleasant or painful experience can withdraw love units, and when a lover is in competition with a spouse, unpleasant experiences are intentionally avoided.

When a spouse is unwilling to break all contact with his/her lover, the betrayed spouse must prepare for what could become a lengthy separation. I recommend it primarily for the protection of the betrayed spouse's emotions, but sometimes the affair itself can make a person so anxiety-ridden that they cling to the straying spouse for security. It just makes the emotional trauma worse, of course, and a counselor is often needed to provide support to make the break. Once the separation is made, a counselor continues to be helpful in reassuring a spouse that they're making the right decision.

A separation is helpful in protecting the emotions of the betrayed spouse. But another reason a separation is helpful is that the betrayed spouse withholds the fulfillment of needs he/she performed prior to the affair. In most cases, a lover meets one or two important emotional needs, and a spouse meets two or three. The wayward spouse comes to realize that the lover cannot meet needs his/her spouse had met and it sometimes leads to the realization that "you can't have your cake and eat it, too." A separation may also result in the opportunity for unpleasant experiences between a spouse and lover, driving down the Love Bank account, but don't count on it!

When the decision is finally made to reconcile and avoid all contact with the lover, it's usually with the hope that the spouse can learn to meet needs met by the lover much more easily than the lover can meet needs met by the spouse. One very important obstacle to leaving a spouse for a lover is children and the extended family. The lover will simply never be able to take the place of the spouse, but the spouse *can* take the place of the lover.

You should expect reality to prevail eventually. But before I explain what to do at that point, let me illustrate what you should expect by examining the story of Alex and Elaine—and Harriet.

The Anatomy of an Affair

Alex sighed quietly as he reached over to turn out the light. Then he turned back to kiss Elaine's cheek. "Good night, honey," he whispered.

No answer. Elaine slept soundly on. That did not surprise him, and he knew how angry she'd be if he woke her just to make love. He lay down and pulled the covers over his shoulder. Long ago he had given up the loser's game of feeling sorry for himself. He just had to face it that Elaine no longer felt any interest in sex. She had once, he'd thought, in the early years of their marriage, before the children came along.

Next morning as Alex caught the 7:30 commuter train he greeted Harriet and Fred, who also worked for his firm. As Alex opened his morning paper he remembered his empty noon schedule.

"Hey, you two," he called out. "My lunch partner's out of town today. Either of you free?"

"Sorry," Fred told him. "I have to be across town."

Alex looked at Harriet, a tall, willowy woman, studious and plain. "I'd love to go to lunch with you," she answered brightly.

I haven't seen her in a while, Alex thought. Harriet had gone to his high school, and they'd lost track of each other for a few years, until they started working for the same company. Their friendship rekindled several months before, when they began working on the same team, installing a new computer system. Once they'd completed that, though,

Alex's responsibilities took him to the fifth floor, while she stayed on the seventh.

"You know," Alex told her that day at lunch, "I'm kind of glad Charlie had to go out of town today."

"Me, too," she agreed, smiling. "I've missed you since you went downstairs. We should have done this sooner."

"Yeah. Working on that project was the most fun I've had in a long time."

"The system's really proving itself, too. Float time on orders has been reduced to almost nothing."

"That doesn't surprise me." Alex chuckled. "Why, with you and me on that job, it *couldn't* fail."

As they left Alex and Harriet made plans to meet again next week. Soon the midweek luncheon had become a regular part of their schedules. Once Harriet gave Alex a book on computer programming, and a few weeks later he responded with a modest but lovely bracelet. As he gave it to her at lunch her face lit up. Leaning over the table, she kissed him gently on the cheek.

"Harriet, I have to be honest," he told her awkwardly. "I'm getting awfully attached to you. It's . . . well, it's more than friendship."

"Alex," she responded, her voice low, "I feel that way, too."

"I've never told you how I feel about Elaine. . . ."

"And you never need to," she reassured him.

"But I want to. I've never been able to talk to anyone about it before. I'd like to now."

"Then go ahead. It's okay."

"When I married her, I didn't realize what I was letting myself in for. I thought we shared a lot of interests, would spend a lot of time together, but all that dried up within a year or so. Now she does her thing, and I do mine. She doesn't like me to talk to her about work, and she complains I don't earn enough money. Half the time, when I get home at night, it's like walking into a madhouse. . . ."

Harriet listened in sympathetic silence; afterwards he stopped in at her place, "to talk."

The next morning, when Alex awakened in Harriet's bed, he thought how pretty she looked. He kissed her bare shoulder and smiled as she opened her eyes. "Hi, handsome," she whispered.

"Hello, beautiful."

After that evening, Alex and Harriet seemed obsessed with each other. Never in his life had Alex experienced such enthusiastic and consistent lovemaking.

At first Elaine only experienced some vague doubts about Alex, but soon her doubts turned to suspicions as his absences increased. The occasional stay in town overnight extended to his leaving the house on weekend afternoons. Finally, one night she decided to test her suspicions and called Jake, with whom Alex said he planned to spend the night. Jake tried to say Alex hadn't arrived yet, but his performance left Elaine unconvinced. When she tried to call later, no one answered the phone.

Elaine remembered hearing Alex talk warmly about working with Harriet on a computer project. She also knew Harriet didn't live too far away and decided she might be a likely prospect. One Saturday afternoon when Alex had disappeared, Elaine hired a neighborhood teenager to watch the children and drove to Harriet's apartment. As soon as she turned onto her block, she spotted Alex's car, parked just around the corner.

Elaine parked, found Harriet's apartment, and took a deep breath as she rang the bell. Harriet answered the door, wearing a dressing gown. "Elaine!" she said just a bit too loudly. "Why, what a surprise—"

"I'm sorry, Harriet, if this seems rude, but I must come in to see something for myself." She brushed past the other woman and walked through the apartment, into the bedroom. There she found Alex, hurriedly pulling on his trousers. The rest of his clothes were still draped over a chair near the bed.

"Elaine! I—"

His wife spun around and walked out of the apartment wordlessly. She saw no signs of Harriet and didn't even bother to close the door on her way out. Once in her car, Elaine burst into tears. As she automatically drove home she attempted to force her numb mind to think. Divorce seemed her only option.

Alex and Harriet stood by the front window and watched Elaine drive away. "What will you do?" Harriet asked.

"I've got to go after her and try to cool her down. Don't worry about it, love. It's going to work out."

When he got home, Alex saw Elaine's car, engine running and door ajar, standing in the driveway. He turned off the ignition, pocketed the key, and closed the door. As he walked through the front door he heard the children crying. The bewildered baby-sitter told him his wife had gone upstairs. He paid her and sent her home, then went to find Elaine. She had locked herself in the bedroom. After calling to her a few times, he realized he'd better take care of the kids first. They went out for some fast food, and he put them to bed. All that time the door to the bedroom remained tightly shut.

Again Alex knocked at the door. No answer. "Elaine, please," he begged softly.

The lock on the knob clicked, and he tried the door again. As it opened he saw Elaine sitting on the bed, eyes swollen and puffy with crying. He walked over to her, "I'm so ashamed, honey—"

"Don't you *dare* call me honey!" she hissed.

"But Elaine, I love you and the children. You mean the world to me. I don't understand how I could have done this to you." Again Elaine started sobbing, and instinctively Alex tried to comfort her.

"Don't touch me!" she gasped, struggling away from him to perch in the middle of the bed. "How could you do that? I hate the sight of you!"

"Elaine, please . . . It'll never happen again. I must have been crazy, please give me another chance." Tears welled up in his eyes.

"You liar! You lied to me about all those nights you had to spend at Jake's, didn't you!?"

"Elaine, please, no—"

"Don't lie. It only makes it worse!"

"You're right, and I won't lie anymore. You've got to believe me! I can only promise you it won't happen again. You and the kids mean too much to me. It's all over, Elaine, I mean it."

This sort of exchange continued until three o'clock in the morning—Alex begging Elaine for mercy and understanding, and Elaine ripping into him with rage and anguish. Finally, driven by exhaustion, she permitted a truce and allowed Alex to come to bed.

During the next few days Alex continued to show remorse and managed to quiet Elaine down somewhat. By the end of the week he had her convinced that temporary insanity caused his fling with Harriet, and it wouldn't happen again.

Alex did stop seeing Harriet for lunch, but he called her at the first opportunity. "I've got to see you, but I don't dare right now. I love you so much—I just don't know what to do. . . ."

"Alex, I love you, too. There'll never be any question of that. But I want you to hold your marriage together. I don't want to cause a divorce."

"Harriet, you're a jewel. Don't worry. I'll give it my best shot. If it ends in divorce, it won't be your fault."

Alex held out for two weeks and then rendezvoused with Harriet for lunch at an out-of-the-way spot. "I can't stop thinking about you and what we have together. I've never had anything like it in my life, and I know I won't ever have it again."

Harriet could only hold Alex's hand and weep. The next week they met at Jake's apartment and resumed the affair with renewed vigor. It seemed as if they had new energy, stored up over the past weeks of separation. After that they got together whenever possible for lunch. Staying in town overnight was out, because Elaine would suspect. One Saturday afternoon, however, Alex couldn't stand it and quietly left for Harriet's apartment. He didn't realize that Elaine had seen him go and had followed. They repeated the whole sorry discovery scene, which left Elaine utterly inconsolable. She ordered Alex out of the house and filed for divorce.

Alex thought about moving in with Harriet but decided against it. Instead, he found a room at the YMCA and sat on his narrow cot, taking stock. He realized he not only missed Elaine and the children, but that he had many other things to think about—being rejected by his family and friends and having to spend large sums of money on lawyers, alimony, and child support. He also thought about his company and their policy concerning affairs and keeping families together. He could lose his job—or at least miss an upcoming promotion.

One evening, about a week after he had moved out, Alex phoned Elaine: "Please give me one more chance. I think our marriage was in trouble long before this thing happened. I know there were things I was trying to ignore and I was wrong to do that. I should have brought it all out in the open with you and a counselor. Elaine, I really want to save our marriage and our family. Will you go to see someone with me?"

At first Elaine didn't know how to reply. Was Alex right? Maybe she was partly to blame. And he did want to see a counselor.

"Okay," she finally responded. "I'll give it a try."

Before the week was out, Alex had moved out of the YMCA and back into the house. He managed one brief conversation with Harriet, telling her he still loved her but could not get a divorce—not yet, anyway.

During counseling sessions, Alex tried to explain his feelings about why he felt the marriage had gone wrong—and why he held resentment against Elaine.

"Alex," said the counselor, "you need to spell out what you thought was wrong. Let's get specific."

Alex got specific and talked about Elaine's indifference to having sex, her lack of interest in his career, and her unwillingness to share in activities he enjoyed. Then he cited the incessant nagging about household problems, even though she had never had to go out and get a job.

As Elaine listened, she began to wonder if perhaps a lot of the problem wasn't really her fault after all.

Then the counselor zeroed in and asked Alex to be totally honest. Was he still in love with Harriet?

"Yes, I am," Alex said in a mixture of shame and defiance. Alex didn't bother to say that he and Harriet had resumed their affair and still spent lunch hours at Jake's apartment. The counselor did not ask.

In the following months Alex managed to remain in counseling and continue his affair with Harriet. He fooled both Elaine and the counselor into believing he was interested in being permanently faithful to his wife. He learned how to be more careful and less impulsive in his frequent meetings with Harriet.

Are Triangles Always Eternal?

Alex, Elaine, and Harriet seem caught in the eternal triangle, and it's not too hard to see how it happened. When Alex and Elaine married, the balances in their Love Bank accounts stood at the usual all-time highs. But as expectations weren't fulfilled and needs weren't met, Alex became vulnerable to someone else who met his important emotional needs. After that first lunch, Harriet's account in Alex's Love Bank mounted rapidly. The affair developed and Alex wound up in love with two women, instead of only one. Now he found himself locked in a prison; he couldn't seem to do without either of them. Each one met some of his emotional needs that were not met by the other.

So where *do* Alex and Elaine—and Harriet—go from here? In my early years of clinical practice a man like Alex could fool me, but as I tried to help couples just like Alex and Elaine I soon detected a distinct pattern. The estranged spouse just couldn't give up the lover. I tried different tacks and approaches, but nothing worked very effectively. I sent errant spouses to retreats to think it over; I brought in their pastors, when possible, for support and moral encouragement. I worked on the assumption that a new *commitment* would change the behavior of men like Alex. Experience proved me wrong.

Finally I hit upon the "total abstinence" concept used with treating alcoholics. If Alex and Elaine came to me today I would set strict rules for Alex never to see Harriet again. To insure that he keep his end of the bargain, I would insist that Alex give Elaine a twenty-four-hour-a-day schedule of his whereabouts. If Alex cries, "Foul!" or "Unfair!" I simply say, "I know this sounds childish and unfair, but we have a very serious problem here. You say you aren't seeing Harriet anymore. Well, if you mean business, you won't have any trouble providing Elaine with a schedule so that she can feel secure about being able to contact you *at any time*. Furthermore, you should call her periodically just to check in now and then."

Does this twenty-four-hour-a-day checking really work? I assure you it works better than simply *trusting* Alex. Admittedly, there is one real drawback in arranging for this kind of checkup system for someone like Alex. Elaine's account in his Love Bank will not rise rapidly when she checks up on him and he has to make check-in calls to her. In fact, initially such actions cause further withdrawals from her Love Bank balance, because Alex will feel annoyed and irritated.

Obviously we must do more than leave Alex feeling as if he has a parole officer. Typically a straying spouse, confronted with this, responds with total depression. He is trying to save his marriage, but he feels miserable. Now, cut off from Harriet—somebody he loves very much and who met some of his most important emotional needs—and with the checkup going, he finds himself trapped.

Step 4: Start Meeting Each Other's Needs

The fourth step in my program for surviving an affair provides the way out of that trap. Elaine must learn to meet the emotional needs

175

that Harriet met. I realize Alex strayed, but Elaine must come to grips with his unfulfilled emotional needs that left him vulnerable.

If all goes well, Elaine will make herself more available to Alex sexually and start joining him in some of his favorite activities. An ideal scenario would find her reading a book about computers and programming to understand better what he does for a living, and to put icing on the cake, she could start giving him more support at home and stop complaining about how he doesn't earn enough money or do enough around the house.

All this could take many weeks and months. Probably Alex hadn't shown Elaine enough affection, and that's why she resisted him sexually. In addition Alex would need some coaching in having conversations with Elaine. Instead of simply judging Elaine for not being interested in his computer world, he would have to learn how to talk to her about *her* interests and feelings. Elaine needed very deeply the quality of conversation Alex had shared with Harriet.

Obviously Elaine's basic female need for honesty and openness has fallen into serious disrepair. Alex will have to work hard and long to regain her trust, but he can do it.

If I counseled Alex and Elaine, I would make a special point to warn Elaine that she has started down a long and bumpy road. In fact at first, she should expect little positive return for her efforts. Elaine should not expect that as a result of all her changes in her behavior Alex would suddenly become more loving, caring, and faithful. In fact, as I mentioned, Alex will initially react with depression. If he honestly described his thoughts, he would tell Elaine he spends a great deal of time thinking about Harriet. Elaine could even expect some lying and deceit on Alex's part for a certain period of time. Alex will feel tempted to try to sneak away to meet Harriet again.

No matter how well Elaine meets Alex's needs, he will remain in love with Harriet for some time to come. Alex and Elaine can rebuild their marriage by beginning to meet each other's five basic needs. They can reignite the flames of their own love, but all their efforts may not completely extinguish the flame of love ignited by Alex's affair with Harriet. It may burn low, but it might never go out completely. Just as an alcoholic remains addicted to alcohol the rest of his life and never dares to touch another drink, Alex will remain vulnerable to Harriet for life and should not see her again.

When I tell a wife that her straying husband will always be vulnerable to his lover, the typical reaction is often one of despair.

"Then why should I stay with him at all?" is the common response.

"Because you love him and you want to survive this ugly mess," I answer. "I don't like telling you this any more than you like hearing it, but I've seen it too many times. You *must* accept the fact that your husband will be vulnerable to the other woman. But that doesn't mean you can't build a stronger love between the two of you."

I've found that breaking a man away from his lover after he reconciles with his wife proves more difficult than breaking a woman away from her lover. I am not sure why this is so. Perhaps women feel more uncomfortable loving two men, while men adjust better to multiple relationships. Throughout history, in the common system of polygamy, men have supported many women, but most societies have not permitted women to do the same. Usually sociologists have assumed this discrimination had an economic base (men could support women, but women could not usually support men), but the reason may also turn out to be emotional—men like having several wives, while women do not like having several husbands.

When a man wins a wife back from an affair by learning to meet her needs, he has little to worry about. My counseling experiences have shown that when a straying wife comes back to her husband and finds her needs being met, her former lover often no longer tempts her.

But with straying husbands we have a more serious problem. I have seen husbands build new and wonderful relationships with their wives but then go back to their lovers after five or six years of what appeared to be marital bliss. When I ask them why, they inevitably tell me they miss the woman terribly and still love her. At the same time they stoutly affirm they love their wives dearly and would not think of leaving them.

I believe a man like this has told the truth. He is hopelessly entangled and needs all the help possible to be kept away from his lover and stay faithful to his wife. I often recommend that a man once involved in an affair come in to see me every three to six months on an indefinite basis, just to talk about how things are going and to let me know how successfully he has stayed away from his lover. He must resign himself to a lifetime without her. He must certainly not work with his former lover and should probably live in some other city or state. Even with those restrictions the desire for her company persists.

Your Marriage Will Become Stronger Than Ever

When you have finally learned to meet each other's most important emotional needs, your love and your marriage will become stronger than ever. A person who discovers his or her spouse in an affair experiences one of the most severe blows anyone's self-esteem could possibly sustain. It also begins a constant struggle that puts both partners on an emotional roller coaster. But once they have weathered the worst, they discover they love each other more than ever. In fact, many couples tell me they have built a better love relationship than they would have had if the affair had not jolted them into constructive action. The affair provides the traumatic trigger that finally gets the couple working on each other's basic needs. Once you start meeting those basic needs, your marriage becomes what it was supposed to have been all along.

In almost every case that I have counseled, when the couple has faithfully stuck to the program I have laid down, they have developed a better relationship than ever before. People say to me they can never love or trust a spouse again after that spouse has strayed away in an affair. I know this is not true. It is a long and difficult process to restore the relationship, but it can be done!

14

FROM INCOMPATIBLE TO IRRESISTIBLE

To conclude, we need to make a brief study of two important words: *incompatible* and *irresistible*.

Within the definition of these words lies the key to understanding and applying this book to your own marriage. According to *The American Heritage Dictionary* the definition of *incompatible* is: "inharmonious; antagonistic." The definition of *irresistible* is: "having an overpowering appeal."

When a husband and wife can't get along, we may describe them as *incompatible*. Yet at one time, we would have called those same two people irresistible to each other. Because they found each other irresistible, they made a lifetime commitment in marriage. Couples start out irresistible and only become incompatible as they leave each other's needs unmet. When someone outside the marriage offers to meet those needs, an affair starts. Then the lover becomes "irresistible."

But giving the lover that title can be misleading. The lover is seldom "totally irresistible." In most affairs he or she meets only some—usually one or two—of the basic needs of the straying spouse. The betrayed spouse still fulfills the other three or four basic needs. As I've tried to show time and again, when the straying spouse is caught in the web of an affair, he or she feels a strong need for both people—the spouse left at home and the lover. The thought of losing either of them seems unbearable.

Some people I counsel manage to bite the bullet and make a choice between the two. Some choose the spouse, and some choose the lover. In either case they move from guilt and shame to grief and pain. They feel and act depressed because the needs once met by the person they chose to leave now go unmet.

For example, when a straying husband chooses to return to his wife, he often feels that he has made some great sacrifice for his family. In most cases he has been forced to give up a satisfying sexual relationship—perhaps the first he had ever known in his life. Any good feelings he may derive from "having done the right thing" do little to lessen his pain or cool his resentment at the loss of what he had in the affair.

If this same straying man chooses his lover, he feels nearly overwhelmed by guilt and shame for having abandoned a wife who has loved and cared for him in many ways. If children are involved, the guilt and shame multiply rapidly. Another lie being spread on TV talk shows and in pop-psych books and articles is that divorce doesn't necessarily damage children. In some exceptional cases a divorce may be the better of two evils—for example when a marriage involves severe alcoholism, child (and wife) abuse, insanity, and so on—but in the vast majority of cases I've counseled, divorce devastates children. To rationalize otherwise is not only stupid, it is cruel.

In my experience, the spouse trapped in an affair comes through the experience relatively healthy when he or she chooses to resolve incompatibility at home and rebuilds the marriage. Those I have counseled who have abandoned their marriage, without an effort to improve it, suffer relentless guilt and miss an opportunity to learn how to have a successful marriage. Many of those individuals see me years later with the same problems cropping up in their marriages to their lovers. By

the time they resolve them, they know they could have used those principles to save their first marriages.

The Cure for Incompatibility: Getting Down to the Full-Time Business of Meeting Each Other's Most Important Emotional Needs

The quickest cure for incompatibility and fastest road to becoming
irresistible lie in meeting each other's most important emotional needs.
Happily married couples are already aware of this principle and have
learned how to make their marriage a full-time priority. But these couples not only put out the effort, they also put their effort in the *right
places*.

I have seen this principle work in many different situations. For
example, I once managed a dating service in the Twin Cities area. A
dating service is designed to help people with common interests and
objectives meet each other. Soon after I opened the service, I began to
see a very real problem. Those who had enrolled—some five hundred—
needed more than just an opportunity to meet each other. Almost without exception these people lacked skills in meeting the needs of others. Yet each of them eagerly sought someone else who would be highly
skilled in meeting *their* needs and who would take care of them. They
complained that they only met selfish and insensitive people. Of course
they could not see their own selfishness and insensitivity.

So I reorganized the dating service. Rather than help my subscribers
meet eligible people, I helped them become eligible people to meet,
developing skills and other qualities that would make them attractive
to the opposite sex.

A number of the dating-service subscribers bought in to my new
concept and took the pains necessary to become skillful in meeting
the needs of other people. For these men and women, my dating service was a roaring success. In fact, they found they no longer needed
a dating service to introduce them to anyone. Their newly acquired
abilities made them attractive to the opposite sex wherever they went.
Many of them married within two years.

I believe our society's failure to train people in meeting the needs
of others—especially the needs of a marriage partner—has caused

much of our high divorce rate. Marriage is not a simple social institution that everyone eventually enters into because he or she "falls in love and lives happily after." As long as we fail to see marriage as a complex relationship that requires special training and abilities to meet the needs of a member of the opposite sex, we will continue to see a discouraging and devastating divorce rate.

Children should be trained at a very young age to learn how to meet the needs and expectations that will be laid on them if and when they enter marriage. There is no reason we must see so many marriages that barely hold together or that drift into affairs.

Much of this book deals with what people call "bad" marriages—those that wind up in affairs and divorce. I have tried to give advice on how to avoid an affair or survive one. But in truth you can also use this advice to take a medium or good marriage and make it into an absolutely outstanding relationship that finds each partner irresistible to the other. Fortunately you need not merely dream about "becoming irresistible," hoping that it happens if and when you find just the right shampoo, deodorant, or perfume. Let's do a quick review of what it takes to be an irresistible man or woman.

The Irresistible Man

Any husband can make himself irresistible to his wife by learning to meet her five most important emotional needs.

1. *Affection.* Her husband tells her that he loves her with words, cards, flowers, gifts, and common courtesies. He hugs and kisses her many times each day, creating an environment of affection that clearly and repeatedly expresses his love for her.
2. *Conversation.* He sets aside time every day to talk to her. They may talk about events in their lives, their children, their feelings, or their plans. But whatever the topic, she enjoys the conversation because it is never judgmental, always informative and constructive. She talks to him as much as she would like, and responds with interest. He is never too busy "to just talk."
3. *Honesty and openness.* He tells her everything about himself, leaving nothing out that might later surprise her. He describes

182

his positive and negative feelings, events of his past, his daily schedule, and his plans for the future. He never leaves her with a false impression and is truthful about his thoughts, feelings, intentions, and behavior.

4. *Financial support.* He assumes the responsibility to house, feed, and clothe the family. If his income is insufficient to provide essential support, he resolves the problem by upgrading his skills to increase his salary. He does not work long hours, keeping himself from his wife and family, but is able to provide necessary support by working a forty- to forty-five-hour week. While he encourages his wife to pursue a career, he does not depend on her salary for family living expenses.

5. *Family commitment.* He commits sufficient time and energy to the moral and educational development of the children. He reads to them, engages in sports with them, and takes them on frequent outings. He reads books and attends lectures with his wife on the subject of child development so that they will do a good job training the children. He and she discuss training methods and objectives until they agree. He does not proceed with any plan of training discipline without her approval. He recognizes that his care of the children is critically important to her.

Whenever a wife finds a husband who exhibits all five qualities, she will find him irresistible. But a note of caution: If he exhibits only four of them, she will still experience a void that will nag persistently and incessantly for fulfillment. When it comes to meeting the five basic needs, batting 800 is not good enough. Every husband must try for 1,000.

The Irresistible Woman

A wife makes herself irresistible to her husband by learning to meet his five most important emotional needs.

1. *Sexual fulfillment.* His wife meets this need by becoming a terrific sexual partner. She studies her own sexual response to recognize and understand what brings out the best in her; then she

shares this information with him, and together they learn to have a sexual relationship that both find repeatedly satisfying and enjoyable.

2. *Recreational companionship.* She develops an interest in the recreational activities he enjoys most and tries to become proficient at them. If she finds she cannot enjoy them, she encourages him to consider other activities that they can enjoy together. She becomes his favorite recreational companion, and he associates her with his most enjoyable moments of relaxation.

3. *Physical attractiveness.* She keeps herself physically fit with diet and exercise, and she wears her hair, makeup, and clothes in a way that he finds attractive and tasteful. He is attracted to her in private and proud of her in public.

4. *Domestic support.* She creates a home that offers him a refuge from the stresses of life. She manages the household responsibilities in a way that encourages him to spend time at home enjoying his family.

5. *Admiration.* She understands and appreciates him more than anyone else. She reminds him of his value and achievements and helps him maintain self-confidence. She avoids criticizing him. She is proud of him, not out of duty, but from a profound respect for the man she chose to marry.

When a man finds a woman who exhibits all five qualities, he will find her irresistible. But again the same note of caution must be sounded for the woman that sounded for the man. If a wife meets only four of her husband's five emotional needs, he will experience a void that can lead to problems. Like her husband, a wife must seek to bat 1,000 in meeting basic needs. Being satisfied with meeting three or four of his basic needs will not make you totally irresistible.

Discover the Most Important Emotional Needs of You and Your Spouse

As I end, you may still remain unsure that the emotional needs I've described are *your* most important needs—or the most important needs of your spouse.

184

In all honesty, I cannot say for certain which of these needs apply to you or your spouse. So I've provided an opportunity for you and your spouse to find out for yourselves.

In appendix A, I have written a short description of each of the ten emotional needs. Then, in appendix B, there is an Emotional Needs Questionnaire for you to complete. The questionnaire will help you determine which of the ten emotional needs are most important to you and your spouse.

The Emotional Needs Questionnaire should be enlarged with a copy machine so that you will have more space to write your answers. And you will need to make two copies of it—one for you and one for your spouse. Before you complete them, be sure to read appendix A so you will be familiar with all ten emotional needs.

On the last page of the Emotional Needs Questionnaire, you have an opportunity to rank all ten needs in order of their importance to you. This final ranking helps your spouse put your emotional needs in perspective. He or she will know where to put the greatest effort to fulfill your happiness if you rank the needs honestly.

Avoid the temptation of putting only *unfulfilled* needs at the top of the list. Some of your most important needs may already be met. Don't use the list simply to get your spouse's attention; use it to accurately describe your needs. Remember, the needs at the top of the list should be those that give you the greatest pleasure when met, and frustrate you the most when unmet.

I have been saying all along in this book that while both men and women share most of the ten basic needs, the order of their priorities is usually opposite. The top five needs for men are the bottom five for women, and the top five for women are the bottom five for men. When you clearly indicate the priority of your need to your spouse, he or she can invest energy and attention where it does you the most good.

Few experiences match falling in love. But many couples fail to realize that love needs constant nurture and care. I've tried to give you some guidelines for providing that care and for building a marriage that can become better and better. It takes hard work and a willingness to learn new skills, but when you've done this, you will have mastered one of life's most valuable lessons.

Both you and your spouse should complete your copies of the questionnaire, to help you both communicate your needs and how you've done in meeting them. With the increased understanding that comes through this communication, I hope you will build a long and successful marriage.

Appendix A

THE MOST IMPORTANT EMOTIONAL NEEDS

Before you complete the Emotional Needs Questionnaire in appendix B, review the following ten most important emotional needs.

Affection

Quite simply, affection is the expression of love. It symbolizes security, protection, comfort, and approval—vitally important ingredients in any relationship. When one spouse is affectionate to the other, the following messages are sent:

1. You are important to me, and I will care for you and protect you.
2. I'm concerned about the problems you face and will be there for you when you need me.

A hug can say those things. When we hug our friends and relatives, we are demonstrating our care for them. And there are other ways to show our affection—a greeting card, an "I love you" note, a bouquet of flowers, holding hands, walks after dinner, back rubs, phone calls, and conversations with thoughtful and loving expressions can all communicate affection.

Affection is, for many, the essential cement of a relationship. Without it many people feel totally alienated. With it they become emotionally bonded. If you feel terrific when your spouse is affectionate and you feel terrible when there is not enough affection, you have the emotional need for affection.

Sexual Fulfillment

We often confuse sex and affection. Affection is an act of love that is nonsexual and can be received from friends, relatives, children, and even pets. However, acts that can show affection, such as hugging and kissing, that are done with a sexual motive are actually sex, not affection.

Most people know whether or not they have a need for sex, but in case there is any uncertainty, I will point out some of the most obvious symptoms.

A sexual need usually predates your current relationship and is somewhat independent of your relationship. While you may have discovered a deep desire to make love to your spouse since you've been in love, it isn't quite the same thing as a sexual need. Wanting to make love when you are in love is sometimes merely a reflection of wanting to be emotionally and physically close.

Sexual fantasies are usually a dead giveaway for a sexual need. Fantasies in general are good indicators of emotional needs—your most common fantasies usually reflecting your most important needs. If you have imagined what it would be like having your sexual need met in the most fulfilling ways, you probably have a sexual need. The more the fantasy is employed, the greater your need. And the way your sexual need is met in your fantasy is usually a good indicator of your sexual predispositions and orientation.

When you married, you and your spouse both promised to be faithful to each other for life. This means that you agreed to be each other's only sexual partner "until death do us part." You made this commitment because you trusted each other to meet your sexual needs, to be sexually available and responsive. The need for sex, then, is a very exclusive need, and if you have it, you will be very dependent on your spouse to meet it for you. You have no other ethical choice.

Conversation

Unlike sex, conversation is not a need that can be met exclusively in marriage. Our need for conversation can be ethically met by almost anyone. But if it is one of your most important emotional needs, whoever meets it best will deposit so many love units, you may fall in love with that person. So if it's your need, be sure that your spouse is the one who meets it the best and most often.

Men and women don't have too much difficulty talking to each other during courtship. That's a time of information gathering for both partners. Both are highly motivated to discover each other's likes and dislikes, personal background, current interests, and plans for the future.

But after marriage many women find that the man who would spend hours talking to her on the telephone, now seems to have lost all interest in talking to her and spends his spare time watching television or reading. If your need for conversation was fulfilled during courtship, you expect it to be met after marriage.

If you see conversation as a practical necessity, primarily as a means to an end, you probably don't have much of a need for it. But if you have a craving just to talk to someone, if you pick up the telephone just because you feel like talking, if you enjoy conversation in its own right, consider conversation to be one of your most important emotional needs.

Recreational Companionship

A need for recreational companionship combines two needs into one: the need to engage in recreational activities and the need to have a companion.

During your courtship, you and your spouse were probably each other's favorite recreational companions. It's not uncommon for women to join men in hunting, fishing, watching football, or other activities they would never choose on their own. They simply want to spend as much time as possible with the man they like and that means going where he goes.

The same is true of men. Shopping centers are not unfamiliar to men in love. They will also take their dates out to dinner, watch romantic movies, and attend concerts and plays. They take every opportunity to be with someone they like and try to enjoy the activity to guarantee more dates in the future.

I won't deny that marriage changes a relationship considerably. But does it have to end the activities that helped make the relationship so compatible? Can't a husband's favorite recreational companion be his wife and vice versa?

If recreational activities are important to you and you like to have someone join you for them to be fulfilling, include recreational companionship on your list of needs. Think about it for a moment in terms of the Love Bank. How much do you enjoy these activities and how many love units would your spouse be depositing whenever you enjoyed them together? What a waste it would be if someone else got credit for all those love units! And if it is someone of the opposite sex, it would be downright dangerous.

Who should get credit for all those love units? The one you should love the most, your spouse. That's precisely why I encourage a husband and wife to be each other's favorite recreational companion. It's one of the simplest ways to deposit love units.

Honesty and Openness

Most of us want an honest relationship with our spouse. But some of us have a need for such a relationship because honesty and openness give us a sense of security.

To feel secure, we want accurate information about our spouse's thoughts, feelings, habits, likes, dislikes, personal history, daily activities, and plans for the future. If a spouse does not provide honest and open communication, trust can be undermined and the feelings of security can eventually be destroyed. We can't trust the signals that are being sent and we have no foundation on which to build a solid relationship. Instead of adjusting to each other, we feel off balance; instead of growing together, we grow apart.

Aside from the practical considerations of honesty and openness, there are some of us who feel happy and fulfilled when our spouse reveals his or her most private thoughts to us. And we feel very frustrated when they are hidden. That reaction is evidence of an emotional need, one that can and should be met in marriage.

An Attractive Spouse

For many people, physical appearance can become one of the greatest sources of love units. If you have this need, an attractive person will not only get your attention, but may distract you from whatever you're doing. In fact, that's what may have first drawn you to your spouse— his or her physical appearance.

There are some who consider this need to be temporary and important only in the beginning of a relationship. After a couple get to know each other better, some feel that physical attractiveness should take a back seat to deeper and more intimate needs.

But that's not been my experience, nor has it been the experience of many people whom I've counseled, particularly men. For many, the need for an attractive spouse continues on throughout marriage, and just seeing the spouse looking attractive deposits love units.

Among the various aspects of physical attractiveness, weight generally gets the most attention. However, choice of clothing, hairstyle, makeup, and personal hygiene also come together to make a person attractive. It can be very subjective, and you are the judge of what is attractive to you.

If the attractiveness of your spouse makes you feel great, and loss of that attractiveness would make you feel very frustrated, you should probably include this category on your list of important emotional needs.

Financial Support

People often marry for the financial security that their spouse provides them. In other words, part of the reason they marry is for money. Is financial support one of your important emotional needs?

It may be difficult for you to know how much you need financial support, especially if your spouse has always been gainfully employed. But what if, before marriage, your spouse had told you not to expect any income from him or her? Would it have affected your decision to marry? Or what if your spouse could not find work, and you had to financially support him or her throughout life? Would that withdraw love units?

You may have a need for financial support if you expect your spouse to earn a living. But you definitely have that need if you do not expect to be earning a living yourself, at least during part of your marriage.

What constitutes financial support? Earning enough to buy everything you could possibly desire or earning just enough to get by? Different couples would answer this differently, and the same couples might answer differently in different stages of life. But, like many of these emotional needs, financial support is sometimes hard to talk about. As a result, many couples have hidden expectations, assumptions, and resentments. Try to understand what you expect from your spouse financially to feel fulfilled. And what would it take for you to feel frustrated? Your analysis will help you determine if you have a need for financial support.

Domestic Support

The need for domestic support is a time bomb. At first it seems irrelevant, a throwback to more primitive times. But for many couples, the need explodes after a few years of marriage, surprising both husband and wife.

Domestic support includes cooking meals, washing dishes, washing and ironing clothes, cleaning house, and child care. If you feel very fulfilled when your spouse does these things and very annoyed when they are not done, you have the need for domestic support.

In earlier generations, it was assumed that all husbands had this need and all wives would naturally meet it. Times have changed, and needs have changed along with them. Now many of the men I counsel would rather have their wives meet their needs for affection or conversation, needs that have traditionally been more characteristic of women. And many women, especially career women, gain a great deal of pleasure having their husbands create a peaceful and well-managed home environment.

Marriage usually begins with a willingness of both spouses to share domestic responsibilities. Newlyweds commonly wash dishes together, make the bed together, and divide many household tasks. The groom welcomes his wife's help in doing what he had to do by himself as a bachelor. At this point in marriage, neither of them would identify domestic support as an important emotional need. But the time bomb is ticking.

When does the need for domestic support explode? When the children arrive! Children create huge needs—both a greater need for income and greater domestic responsibilities. The previous division of labor becomes obsolete. Both spouses must take on new responsibilities—and which ones will they take?

At this point in your marriage, you may find no need for domestic support at all. But that may change later when you have children. In fact, as soon as you are expecting your first child, you will find yourselves dramatically changing your priorities.

Family Commitment

In addition to a greater need for income and domestic responsibilities, the arrival of children creates in many people the need for family commitment. Again, if you don't have children yet, you may not sense this need, but when the first child arrives, a change may take place that you didn't anticipate.

Family commitment is not just child care—feeding, clothing, or watching over children to keep them safe. Child care falls under the category of domestic support. Family commitment, on the other hand, is a responsibility for the development of the children, teaching them the values of cooperation and care for each other. It is spending quality time with your children to help them develop into successful adults.

Evidence of this need is a craving for your spouse's involvement in the educational and moral development of your children. When he or she is helping care for them, you feel very fulfilled, and when he or she neglects their development, you feel very frustrated.

We all want our children to be successful, but if you have the need for family commitment, your spouse's participation in family activities will deposit carloads of love units. And your spouse's neglect of your children will noticeably withdraw them.

Admiration

If you have the need for admiration, you may have fallen in love with your spouse partly because of his or her compliments to you. Some people just love to be told that they are appreciated. Your spouse may also have been careful not to criticize you. If you have a need for admiration, criticism may hurt you deeply.

Many of us have a deep desire to be respected, valued, and appreciated by our spouse. We need to be affirmed clearly and often. There's nothing wrong with feeling that way. Even God wants us to appreciate him!

Appreciation is one of the easiest needs to meet. Just a compliment, and presto, you've made your spouse's day. On the other hand, it's also easy to be critical. A trivial word of rebuke can be very upsetting to some people, ruining their day and withdrawing love units at an alarming rate.

Your spouse may have the power to build up or deplete his or her account in your Love Bank with just a few words. If you can be affected that easily, be sure to add admiration to your list of important emotional needs.

Appendix B

EMOTIONAL NEEDS QUESTIONNAIRE

© 1986 by Willard F. Harley, Jr.

Name_____ Date_____

This questionnaire is designed to help you determine your most important emotional needs and evaluate your spouse's effectiveness in meeting those needs. Answer all the questions as candidly as possible. Do not try to minimize any needs that you feel have been unmet. If your answers require more space, use and attach a separate sheet of paper.

Your spouse should complete a separate Emotional Needs Questionnaire so that you can discover his or her needs and evaluate your effectiveness in meeting those needs.

When you have completed this questionnaire, go through it a second time to be certain your answers accurately reflect your feelings. Do not erase your original answers, but cross them out lightly so that your spouse can see the corrections and discuss them with you.

The final page of this questionnaire asks you to identify and rank five of the ten needs in order of their importance to you. The most important emotional needs are those that give you the most pleasure when met and frustrate you the most when unmet. Resist the temptation to identify as most important only those needs that your spouse is *not* presently meeting. Include *all* your emotional needs in your consideration of those that are most important.

You have the permission of the publisher to photocopy the questionnaire for use in your own marriage. I recommend that you enlarge it 125 percent so that you'll have plenty of room to write in your responses.

1. **Affection.** Showing love through words, cards, gifts, hugs, kisses, and courtesies; creating an environment that clearly and repeatedly expresses love.

   A. **Need for affection:** Indicate how much you need affection by circling the appropriate number.

   ```
   0         1         2         3         4         5         6
   |---------|---------|---------|---------|---------|---------|
   I have no need          I have a moderate          I have a great need
   for affection           need for affection          for affection
   ```

   If or when your spouse is *not* affectionate with you, how do you feel? (Circle the appropriate letter.)
   a. Very unhappy   c. Neither happy nor unhappy
   b. Somewhat unhappy   d. Happy not to be shown affection

   If or when your spouse is affectionate to you, how do you feel? (Circle the appropriate letter.)
   a. Very happy   c. Neither happy nor unhappy
   b. Somewhat happy   d. Unhappy to be shown affection

   B. **Evaluation of spouse's affection:** Indicate your satisfaction with your spouse's affection toward you by circling the appropriate number.

   ```
   -3        -2        -1        0         1         2         3
   |---------|---------|---------|---------|---------|---------|
   I am extremely          I am neither satisfied          I am extremely
   dissatisfied            nor dissatisfied                satisfied
   ```

   My spouse gives me all the affection I need.   Yes   No

   If your answer is no, how often would you like your spouse to be affectionate with you?

   _____ (write number) times each day/week/month (circle one).

   I like the way my spouse gives me affection.   Yes   No

   If your answer is no, explain how your need for affection could be better satisfied in your marriage. _____
   _____
   _____
   _____
   _____
   _____

2. **Sexual Fulfillment.** A sexual relationship that brings out a predictably enjoyable sexual response in both of you that is frequent enough for both of you.

   A. **Need for sexual fulfillment:** Indicate how much you need sexual fulfillment by circling the appropriate number.

0	1	2	3	4	5	6

   I have no need
   for sexual fulfillment

   I have a moderate need
   for sexual fulfillment

   I have a great need
   for sexual fulfillment

   If or when your spouse *is not* willing to engage in sexual relations with you, how do you feel? (Circle the appropriate letter.)
   a. Very unhappy
   b. Somewhat unhappy
   c. Neither happy nor unhappy
   d. Happy not to engage in sexual relations

   If or when your spouse engages in sexual relations with you, how do you feel? (Circle the appropriate letter.)
   a. Very happy
   b. Somewhat happy
   c. Neither happy nor unhappy
   d. Unhappy to engage in sexual relations

   B. **Evaluation of sexual relations with your spouse:** Indicate your satisfaction with your spouse's sexual relations with you by circling the appropriate number.

-3	-2	-1	0	1	2	3

   I am extremely
   dissatisfied

   I am neither satisfied
   nor dissatisfied

   I am extremely
   satisfied

   My spouse has sexual relations with me as often as I need.   Yes   No

   If your answer is no, how often would you like your spouse to have sex with you?

   _____ (write number) times each day/week/month (circle one).

   I like the way my spouse has sexual relations with me.   Yes   No

   If your answer is no, explain how your need for sexual fulfillment could be better satisfied in your marriage. _____
   _____
   _____
   _____

3. **Conversation.** Talking about events of the day, feelings, and plans; avoiding angry or judgmental statements or dwelling on past mistakes; showing interest in your favorite topics of conversation; balancing conversation; using it to inform, investigate, and understand you; and giving you undivided attention.

A. **Need for conversation:** Indicate how much you need conversation by circling the appropriate number.

| 0 | 1 | 2 | 3 | 4 | 5 | 6 |

I have no need
for conversation

I have a moderate need
for conversation

I have a great need
for conversation

If or when your spouse *is not* willing to talk with you, how do you feel? (Circle the appropriate letter.)

a. Very unhappy   c. Neither happy nor unhappy

b. Somewhat unhappy   d. Happy not to talk

If or when your spouse talks to you, how do you feel? (Circle the appropriate letter.)

a. Very happy   c. Neither happy nor unhappy

b. Somewhat happy   d. Unhappy to talk

B. **Evaluation of conversation with your spouse:** Indicate your satisfaction with your spouse's conversation with you by circling the appropriate number.

| -3 | -2 | -1 | 0 | 1 | 2 | 3 |

I am extremely
dissatisfied

I am neither satisfied
nor dissatisfied

I am extremely
satisfied

My spouse talks to me as often as I need.   Yes   No

If your answer is no, how often would you like your spouse to talk to you?

_____ (write number) times each day/week/month (circle one).

_____ (write number) hours each day/week/month (circle one).

I like the way my spouse talks to me.   Yes   No

If your answer is no, explain how your need for conversation could be better satisfied in your marriage. _____

_____

_____

4. **Recreational Companionship.** Developing interest in your favorite recreational activities, learning to be proficient in them, and joining you in those activities. If any prove to be unpleasant to your spouse after an effort has been made, negotiating new recreational activities that are mutually enjoyable.

A. **Need for recreational companionship:** Indicate how much you need recreational companionship by circling the appropriate number.

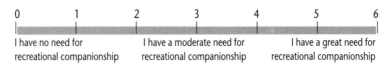

```
0        1        2        3        4        5        6
|--------|--------|--------|--------|--------|--------|
I have no need for         I have a moderate need for      I have a great need for
recreational companionship recreational companionship     recreational companionship
```

If or when your spouse *is not* willing to join you in recreational activities, how do you feel? (Circle the appropriate letter.)

a. Very unhappy   c. Neither happy nor unhappy
b. Somewhat unhappy   d. Happy not to include my spouse

If or when your spouse joins you in recreational activities, how do you feel? (Circle the appropriate letter.)

a. Very happy   c. Neither happy nor unhappy
b. Somewhat happy   d. Unhappy to include my spouse

B. **Evaluation of recreational companionship with your spouse:** Indicate your satisfaction with your spouse's recreational companionship by circling the appropriate number.

```
-3       -2       -1        0        1        2        3
|--------|--------|--------|--------|--------|--------|
I am extremely            I am neither satisfied          I am extremely
dissatisfied             nor dissatisfied                 satisfied
```

My spouse joins me in recreational activities as often as I need.   Y   N

If your answer is no, how often would you like your spouse to join you in recreational activities?

_____ (write number) times each day/week/month (circle one).

_____ (write number) hours each day/week/month (circle one).

I like the way my spouse joins me in recreational activities.   Yes   No

If your answer is no, explain how your need for recreational companionship could be better satisfied in your marriage. _____
_____
_____

5. **Honesty and Openness.** Revealing positive and negative feelings, events of the past, daily events and schedule, plans for the future; not leaving you with a false impression; answering your questions truthfully.

A. **Need for honesty and openness:** Indicate how much you need honesty and openness by circling the appropriate number.

```
 0          1          2          3          4          5          6
 |          |          |          |          |          |          |
```
I have no need   I have a moderate need   I have a great need
for honesty and openness   for honesty and openness   for honesty and openness

If or when your spouse *is not* open and honest with you, how do you feel? (Circle the appropriate letter.)

a. Very unhappy   c. Neither happy nor unhappy
b. Somewhat unhappy   d. Happy that my spouse isn't honest
                            and open

If or when your spouse is open and honest with you, how do you feel? (Circle the appropriate letter.)

a. Very happy   c. Neither happy nor unhappy
b. Somewhat happy   d. Unhappy that my spouse is
                            honest and open

B. **Evaluation of spouse's honesty and openness:** Indicate your satisfaction with your spouse's honesty and openness by circling the appropriate number.

```
-3         -2         -1          0          1          2          3
 |          |          |          |          |          |          |
```
I am extremely   I am neither satisfied   I am extremely
dissatisfied   nor dissatisfied   satisfied

In which of the following areas of honesty and openness would you like to see improvement from your spouse? (Circle the letters that apply to you.)

a. Sharing positive and negative emotional reactions to significant aspects of life
b. Sharing information regarding his/her personal history
c. Sharing information about his/her daily activities
d. Sharing information about his/her future schedule and plans

If you circled any of the above, explain how your need for honesty and openness could be better satisfied in your marriage. _____

_____

_____

6. Attractiveness of Spouse. Keeping physically fit with diet and excercise; wearing hair, clothing, and (if female) makeup in a way that you find attractive and tasteful.

A. Need for an attractive spouse: Indicate how much you need an attractive spouse by circling the appropriate number.

0	1	2	3	4	5	6

I have no need
for an attractive spouse

I have a moderate need
for an attractive spouse

I have a great need
for an attractive spouse

If or when your spouse *is not* willing to make the most of his or her physical attractiveness, how do you feel? (Circle the appropriate letter.)

a. Very unhappy

b. Somewhat unhappy

c. Neither happy nor unhappy

d. Happy he or she does not make an effort

When your spouse makes the most of his physical attractiveness, how do you feel? (Circle the appropriate letter.)

a. Very happy

b. Somewhat happy

c. Neither happy nor unhappy

d. Unhappy to see that he or she makes an effort

B. Evaluation of spouse's attractiveness: Indicate your satisfaction with your spouse's attractiveness by circling the appropriate number.

-3	-2	-1	0	1	2	3

I am extremely
dissatisfied

I am neither satisfied
nor dissatisfied

I am extremely
satisfied

In which of the following characteristics of attractiveness would you like to see improvement from your spouse? (Circle the letters that apply.)

a. Physical fitness and normal weight

b. Attractive choice of clothes

c. Attractive hairstyle

d. Good physical hygiene

e. Attractive facial makeup

f. Other _____

If you circled any of the above, explain how your need for an attractive spouse could be better satisfied in your marriage. _____

_____

_____

_____

_____

7. **Financial Support.** Provision of the financial resources to house, feed, and clothe your family at a standard of living acceptable to you, but avoiding travel and working hours that are unacceptable to you.

    A. **Need for financial support:** Indicate how much you need financial support by circling the appropriate number.

0	1	2	3	4	5	6

I have no need
for financial support

I have a moderate need
for financial support

I have a great need
for financial support

       If or when your spouse *is not* willing to support you financially, how do you feel? (Circle the appropriate letter.)

       a. Very unhappy   c. Neither happy nor unhappy

       b. Somewhat unhappy   d. Happy not to be financially supported

       If or when your spouse supports you financially, how do you feel? (Circle the appropriate letter.)

       a. Very happy   c. Neither happy nor unhappy

       b. Somewhat happy   d. Unhappy to be financially supported

    B. **Evaluation of spouse's financial support:** Indicate your satisfaction with your spouse's financial support by circling the appropriate number.

-3	-2	-1	0	1	2	3

I am extremely
dissatisfied

I am neither satisfied
nor dissatisfied

I am extremely
satisfied

       How much money would you like your spouse to earn to support you?

_____

       How many hours each week would you like your spouse to work? _____

       If your spouse is not earning as much as you would like, is not working the hours you would like, does not budget the way you would like, or does not earn an income the way you would like, explain how your need for financial support could be better satisfied in your marriage. _____

_____
_____
_____
_____
_____

8. **Domestic support.** Creation of a home environment for you that offers a refuge from the stresses of life; managing the home and care of the children—if any are at home—including but not limited to cooking meals, washing dishes, washing and ironing clothes, and housecleaning.

   A. **Need for domestic support:** Indicate how much you need domestic support by circling the appropriate number.

0	1	2	3	4	5	6

   I have no need   I have a moderate need   I have a great need
   for domestic support   for domestic support   for domestic support

   If your spouse *is not* willing to provide you with domestic support, how do you feel? (Circle the appropriate letter.)
   a. Very unhappy   c. Neither happy nor unhappy
   b. Somewhat unhappy   d. Happy not to have domestic support

   If or when your spouse provides you with domestic support, how do you feel? (Circle the appropriate letter.)
   a. Very happy   c. Neither happy nor unhappy
   b. Somewhat happy   d. Unhappy to have domestic support

   B. **Evaluation of spouse's domestic support:** Indicate your satisfaction with your spouse's domestic support by circling the appropriate number.

-3	-2	-1	0	1	2	3

   I am extremely   I am neither satisfied   I am extremely
   dissatisfied   nor dissatisfied   satisfied

   My spouse provides me with all the domestic support I need. Yes No

   I like the way my spouse provides domestic support. Yes No

   If your answer is no to either of the above questions, explain how your need for domestic support could be better satisfied in your marriage. _____
   _____
   _____
   _____
   _____
   _____

9. **Family commitment.** Scheduling sufficient time and energy for the moral and educational development of your children; reading to them, taking them on frequent outings, educating himself or herself in appropriate child-training methods and discussing those methods with you; avoiding any child-training method or disciplinary action that does not have your enthusiastic support.

A. **Need for family commitment:** Indicate how much you need family commitment by circling the appropriate number.

```
0         1         2         3         4         5         6
|—————————|—————————|—————————|—————————|—————————|—————————|
I have no need              I have a moderate need         I have a great need
for family commitment      for family commitment          for family commitment
```

If or when your spouse *is not* willing to provide family commitment, how do you feel? (Circle the appropriate letter.)
a. Very unhappy   c. Neither happy nor unhappy
b. Somewhat unhappy   d. Happy he or she is not involved

If or when your spouse provides family commitment, how do you feel? (Circle the appropriate letter.)
a. Very happy   c. Neither happy nor unhappy
b. Somewhat happy   d. Unhappy he or she is involved in
                                      the family

B. **Evaluation of spouse's family commitment:** Indicate your satisfaction with your spouse's family commitment by circling the appropriate number.

```
-3        -2        -1        0         1         2         3
|—————————|—————————|—————————|—————————|—————————|—————————|
I am extremely             I am neither satisfied          I am extremely
dissatisfied               nor dissatisfied                satisfied
```

My spouse commits enough time to the family.   Yes   No

If your answer is no, how often would you like your spouse to join in family activities?

_____ (write number) times each day/week/month (circle one).

_____ (write number) hours each day/week/month (circle one).

I like the way my spouse spends time with the family.   Yes   No

If your answer is no, explain how your need for family commitment could be better satisfied in your marriage. _____

10. **Admiration.** Respecting, valuing, and appreciating you; rarely critical; and expressing admiration to you clearly and often.

  A. **Need for admiration:** Indicate how much you need admiration by circling the appropriate number.

0	1	2	3	4	5	6

I have no need   I have a moderate need   I have a great need
for admiration   for admiration   for admiration

  If or when your spouse *does not* admire you, how do you feel? (Circle the appropriate letter.)
  a. Very unhappy   c. Neither happy nor unhappy
  b. Somewhat unhappy   d. Happy not to be admired

  If or when your spouse does admire you, how do you feel? (Circle the appropriate letter.)
  a. Very happy   c. Neither happy nor unhappy
  b. Somewhat happy   d. Unhappy to be admired

  B. **Evaluation of spouse's admiration:** Indicate your satisfaction with your spouse's admiration of you by circling the appropriate number.

-3	-2	-1	0	1	2	3

I am extremely   I am neither satisfied   I am extremely
dissatisfied   nor dissatisfied   satisfied

  My spouse gives me all the admiration I need.   Yes   No

  If your answer is no, how often would you like your spouse to admire you?
  _____ (write number) times each day/week/month (circle one).

  I like the way my spouse admires me.   Yes   No

  If your answer is no, explain how your need for admiration could be better satisfied in your marriage. _____
  _____
  _____
  _____
  _____
  _____
  _____

Ranking of Your Emotional Needs

The ten basic emotional needs are listed below. There is also space for you to add other emotional needs that you feel are essential to your marital happiness.

In the space provided before each need, write a number from 1 to 5 that ranks the need's importance to your happiness. Write a 1 before the most important need, a 2 before the next most important, and so on until you have ranked your five most important needs.

To help you rank these needs, imagine that you will have only one need met in your marriage. Which would make you the happiest, knowing that all the others would go unmet? That need should be 1. If only two needs will be met, what would your second selection be? Which five needs, when met, would make you the happiest?

_____ Affection

_____ Sexual Fulfillment

_____ Conversation

_____ Recreational Companionship

_____ Honesty and Openness

_____ Attractiveness of Spouse

_____ Financial Support

_____ Domestic Support

_____ Family Commitment

_____ Admiration

_____ _____

_____ _____

Appendix C

ADDITIONAL FORMS

Recreational Enjoyment Inventory

Please indicate how much you enjoy, or think you might enjoy, each recreational activity listed below. In the space provided by each activity, under the appropriate column (husband's or wife's), circle one of the following numbers to reflect your feelings: 3 = very enjoyable; 2 = enjoyable; 1 = somewhat enjoyable; 0 = no feelings one way or the other; -1 = somewhat unpleasant; -2 = unpleasant; -3 = very unpleasant. Add to the list, in the spaces provided, activities that you would enjoy that are not listed. In the third column, add the ratings of both you and your spouse *only if both ratings are positive*. The activities with the highest sum are those that you should select when planning recreational time together.

Activity	Husband's Rating	Wife's Rating	Total Rating
Acting	−3 −2 −1 0 1 2 3	−3 −2 −1 0 1 2 3	_____
Aerobic exercise	−3 −2 −1 0 1 2 3	−3 −2 −1 0 1 2 3	_____
Amusement parks	−3 −2 −1 0 1 2 3	−3 −2 −1 0 1 2 3	_____
Antique collecting	−3 −2 −1 0 1 2 3	−3 −2 −1 0 1 2 3	_____
Archery	−3 −2 −1 0 1 2 3	−3 −2 −1 0 1 2 3	_____
Astronomy	−3 −2 −1 0 1 2 3	−3 −2 −1 0 1 2 3	_____
Auto customizing	−3 −2 −1 0 1 2 3	−3 −2 −1 0 1 2 3	_____
Auto racing (watching)	−3 −2 −1 0 1 2 3	−3 −2 −1 0 1 2 3	_____
Badminton	−3 −2 −1 0 1 2 3	−3 −2 −1 0 1 2 3	_____
Baseball (watching)	−3 −2 −1 0 1 2 3	−3 −2 −1 0 1 2 3	_____
Baseball (playing)	−3 −2 −1 0 1 2 3	−3 −2 −1 0 1 2 3	_____
Basketball (watching)	−3 −2 −1 0 1 2 3	−3 −2 −1 0 1 2 3	_____
Basketball (playing)	−3 −2 −1 0 1 2 3	−3 −2 −1 0 1 2 3	_____
Bible study	−3 −2 −1 0 1 2 3	−3 −2 −1 0 1 2 3	_____
Bicycling	−3 −2 −1 0 1 2 3	−3 −2 −1 0 1 2 3	_____
Boating	−3 −2 −1 0 1 2 3	−3 −2 −1 0 1 2 3	_____
Bodybuilding	−3 −2 −1 0 1 2 3	−3 −2 −1 0 1 2 3	_____
Bowling	−3 −2 −1 0 1 2 3	−3 −2 −1 0 1 2 3	_____
Boxing (watching)	−3 −2 −1 0 1 2 3	−3 −2 −1 0 1 2 3	_____
Bridge	−3 −2 −1 0 1 2 3	−3 −2 −1 0 1 2 3	_____
Camping	−3 −2 −1 0 1 2 3	−3 −2 −1 0 1 2 3	_____
Canasta	−3 −2 −1 0 1 2 3	−3 −2 −1 0 1 2 3	_____
Canoeing	−3 −2 −1 0 1 2 3	−3 −2 −1 0 1 2 3	_____
Checkers	−3 −2 −1 0 1 2 3	−3 −2 −1 0 1 2 3	_____
Chess	−3 −2 −1 0 1 2 3	−3 −2 −1 0 1 2 3	_____
Church services	−3 −2 −1 0 1 2 3	−3 −2 −1 0 1 2 3	_____
Coin collecting	−3 −2 −1 0 1 2 3	−3 −2 −1 0 1 2 3	_____
Computer programming	−3 −2 −1 0 1 2 3	−3 −2 −1 0 1 2 3	_____
Computer games	−3 −2 −1 0 1 2 3	−3 −2 −1 0 1 2 3	_____
Computer _____	−3 −2 −1 0 1 2 3	−3 −2 −1 0 1 2 3	_____
Concerts (rock music)	−3 −2 −1 0 1 2 3	−3 −2 −1 0 1 2 3	_____
Concerts (classical music)	−3 −2 −1 0 1 2 3	−3 −2 −1 0 1 2 3	_____
Concerts (country music)	−3 −2 −1 0 1 2 3	−3 −2 −1 0 1 2 3	_____

Activity	Husband's Rating	Wife's Rating	Total Rating
Cribbage	−3 −2 −1 0 1 2 3	−3 −2 −1 0 1 2 3	_____
Croquet	−3 −2 −1 0 1 2 3	−3 −2 −1 0 1 2 3	_____
Dancing (ballroom)	−3 −2 −1 0 1 2 3	−3 −2 −1 0 1 2 3	_____
Dancing (square)	−3 −2 −1 0 1 2 3	−3 −2 −1 0 1 2 3	_____
Dancing (rock)	−3 −2 −1 0 1 2 3	−3 −2 −1 0 1 2 3	_____
Dancing (_____)	−3 −2 −1 0 1 2 3	−3 −2 −1 0 1 2 3	_____
Dining out	−3 −2 −1 0 1 2 3	−3 −2 −1 0 1 2 3	_____
Fishing	−3 −2 −1 0 1 2 3	−3 −2 −1 0 1 2 3	_____
Flying (as pilot)	−3 −2 −1 0 1 2 3	−3 −2 −1 0 1 2 3	_____
Flying (as passenger)	−3 −2 −1 0 1 2 3	−3 −2 −1 0 1 2 3	_____
Football (watching)	−3 −2 −1 0 1 2 3	−3 −2 −1 0 1 2 3	_____
Football (playing)	−3 −2 −1 0 1 2 3	−3 −2 −1 0 1 2 3	_____
Gardening	−3 −2 −1 0 1 2 3	−3 −2 −1 0 1 2 3	_____
Genealogical research	−3 −2 −1 0 1 2 3	−3 −2 −1 0 1 2 3	_____
Golf	−3 −2 −1 0 1 2 3	−3 −2 −1 0 1 2 3	_____
Ham radio	−3 −2 −1 0 1 2 3	−3 −2 −1 0 1 2 3	_____
Handball	−3 −2 −1 0 1 2 3	−3 −2 −1 0 1 2 3	_____
Hiking	−3 −2 −1 0 1 2 3	−3 −2 −1 0 1 2 3	_____
Hockey (watching)	−3 −2 −1 0 1 2 3	−3 −2 −1 0 1 2 3	_____
Hockey (playing)	−3 −2 −1 0 1 2 3	−3 −2 −1 0 1 2 3	_____
Horseback riding	−3 −2 −1 0 1 2 3	−3 −2 −1 0 1 2 3	_____
Horse shows (watching)	−3 −2 −1 0 1 2 3	−3 −2 −1 0 1 2 3	_____
Horse racing	−3 −2 −1 0 1 2 3	−3 −2 −1 0 1 2 3	_____
Horseshoe pitching	−3 −2 −1 0 1 2 3	−3 −2 −1 0 1 2 3	_____
Hot air ballooning	−3 −2 −1 0 1 2 3	−3 −2 −1 0 1 2 3	_____
Hunting	−3 −2 −1 0 1 2 3	−3 −2 −1 0 1 2 3	_____
Ice fishing	−3 −2 −1 0 1 2 3	−3 −2 −1 0 1 2 3	_____
Ice skating	−3 −2 −1 0 1 2 3	−3 −2 −1 0 1 2 3	_____
Jogging	−3 −2 −1 0 1 2 3	−3 −2 −1 0 1 2 3	_____
Judo	−3 −2 −1 0 1 2 3	−3 −2 −1 0 1 2 3	_____
Karate	−3 −2 −1 0 1 2 3	−3 −2 −1 0 1 2 3	_____
Knitting	−3 −2 −1 0 1 2 3	−3 −2 −1 0 1 2 3	_____
Metalwork	−3 −2 −1 0 1 2 3	−3 −2 −1 0 1 2 3	_____

Activity	Husband's Rating	Wife's Rating	Total Rating
Model building	−3 −2 −1 0 1 2 3	−3 −2 −1 0 1 2 3	_____
Monopoly	−3 −2 −1 0 1 2 3	−3 −2 −1 0 1 2 3	_____
Mountain climbing	−3 −2 −1 0 1 2 3	−3 −2 −1 0 1 2 3	_____
Movies	−3 −2 −1 0 1 2 3	−3 −2 −1 0 1 2 3	_____
Museums	−3 −2 −1 0 1 2 3	−3 −2 −1 0 1 2 3	_____
Opera	−3 −2 −1 0 1 2 3	−3 −2 −1 0 1 2 3	_____
Painting	−3 −2 −1 0 1 2 3	−3 −2 −1 0 1 2 3	_____
Photography	−3 −2 −1 0 1 2 3	−3 −2 −1 0 1 2 3	_____
Pinochle	−3 −2 −1 0 1 2 3	−3 −2 −1 0 1 2 3	_____
Plays	−3 −2 −1 0 1 2 3	−3 −2 −1 0 1 2 3	_____
Poetry (writing)	−3 −2 −1 0 1 2 3	−3 −2 −1 0 1 2 3	_____
Polo (watching)	−3 −2 −1 0 1 2 3	−3 −2 −1 0 1 2 3	_____
Pool (or billiards)	−3 −2 −1 0 1 2 3	−3 −2 −1 0 1 2 3	_____
Quilting	−3 −2 −1 0 1 2 3	−3 −2 −1 0 1 2 3	_____
Racquetball	−3 −2 −1 0 1 2 3	−3 −2 −1 0 1 2 3	_____
Remodeling (home)	−3 −2 −1 0 1 2 3	−3 −2 −1 0 1 2 3	_____
Rock collecting	−3 −2 −1 0 1 2 3	−3 −2 −1 0 1 2 3	_____
Roller-skating	−3 −2 −1 0 1 2 3	−3 −2 −1 0 1 2 3	_____
Rowing	−3 −2 −1 0 1 2 3	−3 −2 −1 0 1 2 3	_____
Rummy	−3 −2 −1 0 1 2 3	−3 −2 −1 0 1 2 3	_____
Sailing	−3 −2 −1 0 1 2 3	−3 −2 −1 0 1 2 3	_____
Sculpting	−3 −2 −1 0 1 2 3	−3 −2 −1 0 1 2 3	_____
Shooting (skeet, trap)	−3 −2 −1 0 1 2 3	−3 −2 −1 0 1 2 3	_____
Shooting (pistol)	−3 −2 −1 0 1 2 3	−3 −2 −1 0 1 2 3	_____
Shopping (clothes)	−3 −2 −1 0 1 2 3	−3 −2 −1 0 1 2 3	_____
Shopping (groceries)	−3 −2 −1 0 1 2 3	−3 −2 −1 0 1 2 3	_____
Shopping (vehicles)	−3 −2 −1 0 1 2 3	−3 −2 −1 0 1 2 3	_____
Shopping (_____)	−3 −2 −1 0 1 2 3	−3 −2 −1 0 1 2 3	_____
Shuffleboard	−3 −2 −1 0 1 2 3	−3 −2 −1 0 1 2 3	_____
Sightseeing	−3 −2 −1 0 1 2 3	−3 −2 −1 0 1 2 3	_____
Singing	−3 −2 −1 0 1 2 3	−3 −2 −1 0 1 2 3	_____
Skiing (water)	−3 −2 −1 0 1 2 3	−3 −2 −1 0 1 2 3	_____
Skiing (downhill)	−3 −2 −1 0 1 2 3	−3 −2 −1 0 1 2 3	_____

Activity	Husband's Rating	Wife's Rating	Total Rating
Skiing (cross-country)	−3 −2 −1 0 1 2 3	−3 −2 −1 0 1 2 3	_____
Skin diving (snorkeling)	−3 −2 −1 0 1 2 3	−3 −2 −1 0 1 2 3	_____
Skydiving	−3 −2 −1 0 1 2 3	−3 −2 −1 0 1 2 3	_____
Snowmobiling	−3 −2 −1 0 1 2 3	−3 −2 −1 0 1 2 3	_____
Softball (watching)	−3 −2 −1 0 1 2 3	−3 −2 −1 0 1 2 3	_____
Softball (playing)	−3 −2 −1 0 1 2 3	−3 −2 −1 0 1 2 3	_____
Spearfishing	−3 −2 −1 0 1 2 3	−3 −2 −1 0 1 2 3	_____
Stamp collecting	−3 −2 −1 0 1 2 3	−3 −2 −1 0 1 2 3	_____
Surfing	−3 −2 −1 0 1 2 3	−3 −2 −1 0 1 2 3	_____
Swimming	−3 −2 −1 0 1 2 3	−3 −2 −1 0 1 2 3	_____
Table tennis	−3 −2 −1 0 1 2 3	−3 −2 −1 0 1 2 3	_____
Taxidermy	−3 −2 −1 0 1 2 3	−3 −2 −1 0 1 2 3	_____
Television	−3 −2 −1 0 1 2 3	−3 −2 −1 0 1 2 3	_____
Tennis	−3 −2 −1 0 1 2 3	−3 −2 −1 0 1 2 3	_____
Tobogganing	−3 −2 −1 0 1 2 3	−3 −2 −1 0 1 2 3	_____
Video games	−3 −2 −1 0 1 2 3	−3 −2 −1 0 1 2 3	_____
Video production	−3 −2 −1 0 1 2 3	−3 −2 −1 0 1 2 3	_____
Video movies (watching)	−3 −2 −1 0 1 2 3	−3 −2 −1 0 1 2 3	_____
Volleyball	−3 −2 −1 0 1 2 3	−3 −2 −1 0 1 2 3	_____
Weaving	−3 −2 −1 0 1 2 3	−3 −2 −1 0 1 2 3	_____
Woodworking	−3 −2 −1 0 1 2 3	−3 −2 −1 0 1 2 3	_____
Wrestling (watching)	−3 −2 −1 0 1 2 3	−3 −2 −1 0 1 2 3	_____
Yachting	−3 −2 −1 0 1 2 3	−3 −2 −1 0 1 2 3	_____
_____	−3 −2 −1 0 1 2 3	−3 −2 −1 0 1 2 3	_____
_____	−3 −2 −1 0 1 2 3	−3 −2 −1 0 1 2 3	_____
_____	−3 −2 −1 0 1 2 3	−3 −2 −1 0 1 2 3	_____
_____	−3 −2 −1 0 1 2 3	−3 −2 −1 0 1 2 3	_____
_____	−3 −2 −1 0 1 2 3	−3 −2 −1 0 1 2 3	_____
_____	−3 −2 −1 0 1 2 3	−3 −2 −1 0 1 2 3	_____
_____	−3 −2 −1 0 1 2 3	−3 −2 −1 0 1 2 3	_____
_____	−3 −2 −1 0 1 2 3	−3 −2 −1 0 1 2 3	_____
_____	−3 −2 −1 0 1 2 3	−3 −2 −1 0 1 2 3	_____
_____	−3 −2 −1 0 1 2 3	−3 −2 −1 0 1 2 3	_____
_____	−3 −2 −1 0 1 2 3	−3 −2 −1 0 1 2 3	_____

Activity	Husband's Rating	Wife's Rating	Total Rating
_____	−3 −2 −1 0 1 2 3	−3 −2 −1 0 1 2 3	_____
_____	−3 −2 −1 0 1 2 3	−3 −2 −1 0 1 2 3	_____
_____	−3 −2 −1 0 1 2 3	−3 −2 −1 0 1 2 3	_____
_____	−3 −2 −1 0 1 2 3	−3 −2 −1 0 1 2 3	_____
_____	−3 −2 −1 0 1 2 3	−3 −2 −1 0 1 2 3	_____
_____	−3 −2 −1 0 1 2 3	−3 −2 −1 0 1 2 3	_____
_____	−3 −2 −1 0 1 2 3	−3 −2 −1 0 1 2 3	_____
_____	−3 −2 −1 0 1 2 3	−3 −2 −1 0 1 2 3	_____
_____	−3 −2 −1 0 1 2 3	−3 −2 −1 0 1 2 3	_____
_____	−3 −2 −1 0 1 2 3	−3 −2 −1 0 1 2 3	_____
_____	−3 −2 −1 0 1 2 3	−3 −2 −1 0 1 2 3	_____

Financial Support Inventory: Needs and Wants Budget

This budget is designed to help clarify the need for financial support. The spouse with this need is to complete this questionnaire.

Please create three budgets in the spaces provided under the three columns. Under the Needs Budget column, indicate the monthly cost of meeting the necessities of your life, items you would be uncomfortable without. In the Income section, only your spouse's income should appear in the column.

Under the Wants Budget column, indicate the cost of meeting your needs and your wants—reasonable desires that would be more costly than necessities. These desires should be as realistic as possible. They should not include a new house, a new car, or luxuries unless you have been wanting these items for some time. Both your income and your spouse's income should appear in this column.

The Affordable Budget column should include all the Needs amounts and only the Wants amounts that can be covered by you and your spouse's income. In other words, your income should equal your expenses, and the Income Minus Expenses item at the end of the Affordable Budget column should be zero. This Affordable Budget should be used to guide your household finances if both you and your spouse have agreed to the amounts listed.

Payments from the past few months (or year if possible) will help you arrive at correct estimates. Use monthly averages for items that are not paid monthly, such as repairs, vacations, and gifts. Some items, such as your mortgage payment, will be the same amount for both your Needs and Wants budgets. Other items, such as vacation expense, will be much more a Want than a Need. It is highly recommended that you include in your Needs Budget an emergency expense item that is 10 percent of your total budget. In months with no emergency expenses, it should be saved for the future. Most households suffer needless financial stress when they fail to budget for inevitable emergencies. If you can think of other significant expenses, include these in the blank spaces provided.

If your spouse's income is equal to or greater than the total expenses in the Needs Budget column, it's sufficient to pay for your Needs, and it's meeting your need for financial support. It may actually be covering some of your Wants as well. That may not have been obvious, since you have not been dividing your bills into Needs and Wants. Your need for financial support is still being met when your income is used to pay for Wants that are not covered by your spouse's income.

However, if your spouse's income is insufficient to pay for your Needs, either you must reduce your household expenses without sacrificing your basic needs, or he must increase his income with a pay raise, a new job, or a new career to meet these needs.

Household Expenses and Income	Needs Budget	Wants Budget	Affordable Budget

Expenses

Taxes

    Income tax

    Property tax

    Other taxes

Interest

    Mortgage interest

    Credit card interest

    Automobile loan interest

    Other interest

Insurance

    Homeowner's insurance

    Life insurance

    Liability insurance

    Auto insurance

    Medical and dental insurance

    Other insurance

Home Expenses

    Home repair

    Home remodeling

    Home security

    Home cleaning

    Yard maintenance

    Fuel (gas and electricity)

    Telephone

    Garbage removal

Household Expenses and Income	Needs Budget	Wants Budget	Affordable Budget

Other Home Expenses

Furniture and Appliances

    Furniture purchase

    Appliance purchase

    Furniture and appliance repair

Automobiles

    Husband's auto depreciation

    Husband's auto fuel

    Husband's auto maintenance

    Wife's auto depreciation

    Wife's auto fuel

    Wife's auto maintenance

    Other auto expenses

Food and Entertainment

    Groceries

    Dining out

    Vacation

    Recreational boat expense

    Photography

    Magazines and newspapers

    Cable TV

    Other food and entertainment

Health

    Medical (over insurance)

    Dental (over insurance)

Household Expenses and Income	Needs Budget	Wants Budget	Affordable Budget

Other Home Expenses (continued)

Health (continued)

Nonprescription drugs _____ _____ _____

Exercise expense _____ _____ _____

Special diet expense _____ _____ _____

Other health expenses _____ _____ _____

Clothing

Husband's clothing purchases _____ _____ _____

Wife's clothing purchases _____ _____ _____

Children's clothing purchases _____ _____ _____

Dry cleaning _____ _____ _____

Alterations and repairs _____ _____ _____

Other clothing expenses _____ _____ _____

Personal

Husband's allowance _____ _____ _____

Wife's allowance _____ _____ _____

Children's allowances _____ _____ _____

Gifts

Religious contributions
(tithe, religious organizations) _____ _____ _____

Nonreligious contributions
(other charitable causes) _____ _____ _____

Gifts for special events
(birthdays, Christmas, etc.) _____ _____ _____

Pets

Pet food _____ _____ _____

Veterinary expense _____ _____ _____

Other pet expense _____ _____ _____

Household Expenses and Income	Needs Budget	Wants Budget	Affordable Budget

Other Home Expenses (continued)

Savings

    Savings for children's education

    Savings for retirement (IRAs)

    Savings for other projects

Other Household Expenses

    Banking

    Legal

    Accounting and tax preparation

    Emergency fund (10%)

    _____

Total Household Expenses

Income

    Husband's salary

    Husband's other income

    Wife's salary

    Wife's other income

    Investment income

    Interest income

    _____

Total Household Income

Income Minus Expenses

ABOUT THE AUTHOR

Willard F. Harley, Jr., Ph.D., is a clinical psychologist and marriage counselor. Over the past twenty-five years he has helped thousands of couples overcome marital conflict and restore their love for each other. His innovative counseling methods are described in the books and articles he writes. *His Needs, Her Needs* has been a best-seller since it was published in 1986 and has been translated into German, French, Dutch, and Chinese. Dr. Harley also leads training workshops for couples and marriage counselors and has appeared on hundreds of radio and television programs.

Willard Harley and Joyce, his wife of over thirty years, live in White Bear Lake, Minnesota. They are the parents of two married children who are also marriage counselors.

Dr. Harley would be delighted to hear from you. His web site is:
http://www.marriagebuilders.com

THINK ROMANCE IS IMPOSSIBLE WITH KIDS UNDERFOOT?

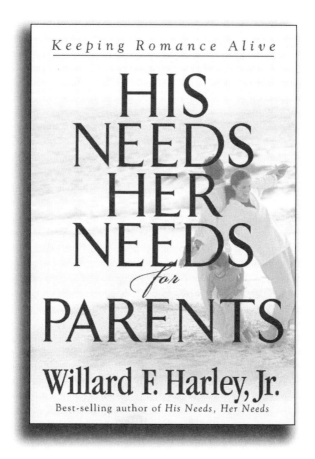

One of the most important things parents can do for their children is keep their marriage healthy. But who can focus on romance when there's parenting to do? Let marriage expert Dr. Willard Harley show you how to sustain a vibrant marriage during the child-rearing years.

*Enjoy a **romantic**, **passionate**, **lifelong** marriage!*
Discover how to meet each other's needs, avoid habits that
chip away at love, and master the art of negotiating.

Whether you know it or not, whether you believe it or not, your marriage depends on the love you and your spouse have for each other. Dr. Harley has spent more than thirty years helping couples create, re-create, and sustain romantic love. In this book, he provides you with all the tools you'll need to fall in love and stay in love with your spouse.

Unabridged audio CD also available. 360 minutes.

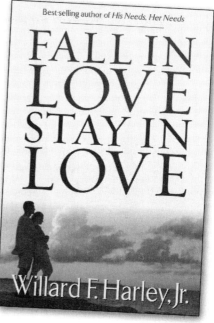

Is the honeymoon over?
Are you losing the love
you once felt for each other?

You've got your fire insurance, your life insurance, your car insurance. Now it's time for marriage insurance. Dr. Harley shares the secrets to a successful marriage. This book will help you identify and overcome the six most common destructive habits that threaten a marriage.

A helpful workbook containing all the contracts, questionnaires, inventories, and worksheets Dr. Harley recommends in *Love Busters* and *His Needs, Her Needs.*

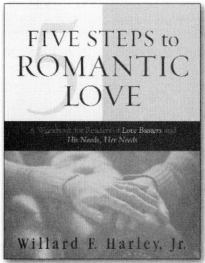

Give others the knowledge to build a lifelong, romantic love! *I Cherish You* highlights the concepts of *His Needs, Her Needs* in a beautiful gift format—perfect for celebrating a wedding or anniversary, or just to say "I love you."

A guide to understanding and surviving every aspect of infidelity—from the beginning of an affair through the restoration of a marriage.

MARRIAGE BUILDERS®

Building Marriages To Last A Lifetime

Dr. Harley has saved thousands of marriages from the pain of unre-solved conflict and the disaster of divorce. His successful approach to building marriages can help you too.

Why do people fall in love? Why do they fall out of love? What do they want most in marriage? What drives them out of marriage? How can a bad marriage become a great marriage? Dr. Harley's basic concepts address these and other important aspects of marriage building.

At www.marriagebuilders.com Dr. Harley introduces visitors to some of the best ways to overcome marital conflicts and some of the quickest ways to restore love. From the pages of "Basic Concepts" and articles by Dr. Harley to the archives for his weekly Q&A columns and information about upcoming seminars, this site is packed with useful material.

Let Marriage Builders™ help you build a marriage to last a lifetime!
www.marriagebuilders.com